Stepping Out in Faith
One Slat at a Time

Stepping Out in Faith
One Slat at a Time

§

Elizabeth Taylor Moulin

LICENSED PROFESSIONAL COUNSELOR
LICENSED MARRIAGE & FAMILY THERAPIST
CERTIFIED SPIRITUAL DIRECTOR/TRAINER
RETREAT DIRECTOR/TRAINER

FOREWORD BY JOSEPH A. TETLOW, S.J.

ISBN: 1519148356
ISBN 13: 9781519148353
Library of Congress Control Number: 2015918506
CreateSpace Independent Publishing Platform
North Charleston, South Carolina

Foreword

§

WHEN LIZ TAYLOR AND ROBERT Moulin went on their honeymoon, the Second Vatican Council was doing its last year of work. The two had been thoroughly formed in the disciplines of the Catholic faith – disciplines that were being challenged by the Council. The upshot of this historical moment is that Liz and Bob lived the unfolding of their successful marriage during the unravelling of ghetto American Catholicism.

You get a feel for what it was like as Liz looks back over those years with a shrewd eye. She sees failures and foibles in clear light and in all their dimensions. She names accurately and vividly the things that hurt. You won't find here much about the public affairs of the times; Liz keeps her focus on her family. But around every paragraph, the Church of the second millennium is ending and the Church – now the People of God – is striking out into the third millennium. Liz goes through ministries and becomes a sought-after spiritual director; Bob does the work of a volunteer chaplain in the hospital ministry.

You will find steady remarks about God's being in the Moulin family's life, and even steadier remarks about God's walking day by day with Liz. This story is the golden thread that runs through the tapestry of relationships intimate and professional, and events familial and medical.

The golden thread of God's Providence highlights Liz's inexhaustible zeal to acquire new learning and new skills. It is clear that she brought this zeal to the discovery of the Ignatian *magis* – the greater and better good – because she is steadily reaching for it.

You might be taken aback at the medical detail in later pages but remember that this is where life takes us, or some of us. Just let it sharpen your appreciation for the courage these trials elicit in the story of Liz's stepping out. In the last analysis, this is the story of a faith that had a surprising beginning and that became more and more surprising as the story unfolded. It is a vivid and surprising instance of what Pope Francis calls *middle-class holiness.*

Among the chattering class, "middle class" is a pejorative. But among the more discerning, it is about as pejorative as "fresh air" or "sunny day." Middle class holiness includes those whom the Mass names "the many" for whom Jesus poured out His blood. And of whom Pope Francis says in his blunt way that "every person is *immensely holy* and deserves our love."

Pope Francis prefaces that with his realism: "Appearances notwithstanding," for all too many people appear to be the opposite of holy. But in this story, appearances not only do not stand in the way, but illustrate Christian holiness. The lives Liz is describing here, starting with her own and her spouse's, manifest the holiness that is given to those who have been baptized into Christ's life and resurrection. This holiness does not make any of us look like the images of saints with their teary eyes staring into the skies. This holiness does not make us look much different from anyone else.

It's only in the unfolding story that you see the difference. Faith instead of pride. Trust in God instead of fierce fight for security. Fidelity in place of self-interest. Wisdom in place of cleverness and cunning. And above all, joy in place of sadness and confusion. You'll find it quite a story.

Joe Tetlow, S.J.
Our Lady of the Oaks at Grand Coteau, Louisiana

Table of Contents

Foreword v

Acknowledgements ix

Preface. xi

Chapter 1   Birth and Family History. 1

Chapter 2   My Mama 6

Chapter 3   My Daddy 17

Chapter 4   My School Years 27

Chapter 5   My Working Career 35

Chapter 6   Marriage & Children 40

Chapter 7   Transfer to Dallas – Lisa's Surgery 55

Chapter 8   From Kindergarten Teacher to College Student. 62

Chapter 9   Special Education Teacher 69

Chapter 10   Breast Cancer & Cancer Work. 77

Chapter 11   Lightning Strikes a Second Time 87

Chapter 12   Adult Children, Marriages,
                     Grandchildren & Great-Grandchildren 91

Chapter 13   Spiritual Direction Training & Retreat Work 114

Chapter 14   My Spiritual Journey 120

Chapter 15   Challenges – Stepping Out in Faith. 130

                     About the Author 143

                     Reviews of the Book 145

Acknowledgements

§

THERE ARE SO MANY PEOPLE who have played a part in my life's journey. I am so grateful to the Sisters of Mount Carmel, especially Sr. Christina Marie Griggs, Sr. "B" DeRouen, my dear friends for 68 years; Mother Angela, Sr. Augusta Marie, Mother Marcella, and Sr. Carmelita, who were my High School teachers at Mt. Carmel Academy and my surrogate family, who loved me and encouraged me on my journey to become a Godly woman and are my angels in Heaven. I am grateful for Marmee Verheugen, my surrogate mother; Julie Verheugen Rozas, my best childhood friend who is a sister to me; my first Mentor, Fr. Sam Anthony Morello, OCD; Fr. Walter McCauley, S.J., my dear friend and former Spiritual Director, who looks down on me from Heaven; Fr. Joe Tetlow, S.J., my dear friend and colleague from whom I have learned so much; Fr. Billy Huete, S.J., my current Spiritual Director, who shares his wisdom and guidance with me; Fr. Bruce Bradley, my dear friend and former Pastor; my dear friend and Prayer Partner Pat Bianco, who so graciously edited my book; my dear friend and colleague Dr. Linda Carmicle; the Director of Montserrat, Ron Boudreaux, S.J., who so generously invites me to retreat work; to all those who encouraged me to write my story; to all those who read my book and graciously wrote testimonials after reading my first draft; and to all my Jesuit Retreat Masters who have helped me on my journey for 45 years. I also want to acknowledge the tremendous impact that watching Joyce Meyer for many years has had on my spiritual journey. I have learned so much from her. I thank God for all who have touched my life!

Without the love and support of my precious family – my loving husband Bob, my loving children and their spouses, my delightful grandchildren and their spouses and my terrific great-grandchildren – I would not have become the person I am today. I am so grateful for their constant encouragement, support and love through the years. God has blessed me abundantly through them!

Preface

§

SINCE I STARTED GIVING TALKS 35 years ago and retreats for the past 17 years, people have been encouraging me to write my story. I have not done anything extraordinary in my life, but what is extraordinary about my life is the way God has worked in it and brought me through so many trials and tribulations. That is my purpose for writing "My Story." I want others to see God's mercy and goodness – to know that no matter what you may go through in life, His grace, wisdom and courage are there to help you! I am in awe of how God's grace is available in the darkest times. His love and comfort are always available to us no matter what is going on that seems so painful, so scary, so insurmountable! If nothing else, my prayer is that my readers will see the power and glory in our awesome God and feel encouraged and inspired to keep on keepin' on – no matter what!

The title for this book came from my painting on the cover. We were in Canada up in the mountains. There was a rope bridge going across a chasm. I was too frightened to cross it, so I watched as others went across. I began to think of the rope bridge as life and how slats could be missing and it would take faith to cross the missing slat. I still could not get on the bridge, but I realized that there had been many bridges in my life and God has always supplied the grace to lift my foot for the next slat. A short time later I was on Retreat with Sr. Marie Schwan at Montserrat where she said that an older

Sister had said that life is like being on a rope bridge with no slats in front of you until you lift your leg to step out in faith. Then God sends an angel with the next slat. I knew then that I had to paint that picture from my head. I am so grateful for that inspiration and affirmation. I have spent my life "Stepping Out in Faith One Slat at a Time."

Dedication

I dedicate this book to my loving Lord, who sustains me in my daily walk with Him and to my precious family who make me so grateful to be a wife, mother, grandmother and great-grandmother!

Chapter 1

House where I was born - 1934

Chapter 1

Me at 1 yr. old

Elizabeth Jeannette Taylor 7 mos. old

Me at 3 yrs. old

Me, Molly + Carolyn
4 yrs. old - 1938

Birth and Family History

§

"It was you who created my inmost self, and put me together
in my mother's womb; for all these mysteries I thank you;
for the wonder of myself, for the wonder of your works."

(*JERUSALEM BIBLE*, PSALM 139:13-14)

THE TERRIFIED CHILD LAY IN her bed as she listened to the horrible accusations her father was shouting at her mother. She wondered if she
should yell at him to stop. She had witnessed many scenes of her drunken
father slapping her mother around and calling her horrible names, some
of which the child did not know the meaning. Finally the yelling stopped.
The sound she heard now was the sound of her mother sobbing. Her first
thought was to comfort her mother, but fear kept her from going into
their bedroom. She wondered why the man who had so graciously helped
her with her homework earlier that evening could become so violent. She
loved her "Daddy" but hated the man he turned into when he was drunk.
The only thing she thought that she could do was to ask the God she had
come to know in religion class to protect her "Mama" and to help her
"Daddy" stop drinking. She also asked God why she was born into this
family – a question she continued to ask for several years to come. That
little child was me and this is my story!

I don't remember this, but my first encounter with a human being, other than my mother's womb, was Dr. Gelpi pulling me through the birth canal, then slapping me on my bottom so that I would cry. That is what doctors did in those days. What a way to welcome a newborn into this world! It was a Tuesday, August 21, 1934. I was born in my parents' bedroom in the house my father built in Westwego, Louisiana, across the river from New Orleans. I was the fifth child born to Georgia Jeannette Mullet Taylor and Albert Seymour Taylor, Jr. My eldest brother Charlie was 22 years old; followed by my brother George, 20 years old; my sister Ruth, 16 years old; and my brother Earl, 14 years old. The boys wanted a baby brother, but my sister Ruth was delighted that I was a girl. My mother was 41 years old and my father was 51 years old. The story I was told is that my mother thought she was going through "the change" and the doctor thought she had a tumor, yeah, a growing tumor! It seems that my existence was denied from the very beginning. What a surprise when my mother felt that tumor kick!

My Daddy told me his version of how I came to them. He said that he heard a baby crying in a refrigerated banana boxcar on his train, so he opened it up and there I was wrapped in a blanket. He said he took me home to Mama. Every time I saw a yellow banana boxcar I would ask my parents if that was the one I was found in. My Daddy would say, "Yes!" The confusion came when there was more than one yellow boxcar. I believed that story during my early years of life.

My earliest memory is sitting in a high chair in my mother's old-fashioned kitchen while she mashed sweet potatoes to feed me. She always put butter, sugar and cinnamon on sweet potatoes – a dish I enjoy till this day. I was wearing maroon corduroy overalls and a white sweater. I suppose I was between two and three years old at the time. Our kitchen was heated by the oven door being left open. I remember how I walked way around that oven door and said, "Hot, don't touch!" I was told that I was very verbal at a very early age – a trait I carry with me to this day.

I slept in a white metal crib in my parents' bedroom. I remember getting a new bed when I was close to three years old. My mother put chairs

2

on the side so that I would not fall out. The other side of the bed was against the wall. The bed was in my parents' bedroom where I slept until I was 8 years old. That bed had great significance as you will see later on in my story.

When I was a baby, Charlie and George made a box to fit on the seat of the wrecker they drove from the service station where they worked. My mother put a pillow and blanket in it so that my brothers could take me with them sometimes. So, my first rides were in a wrecker. Later on I do remember sitting in the backseat of a Model "A" Ford as my mother drove my father to work. Little did I know that I would be driving that Model "A" as a fourteen year old.

Another very vivid memory is that of a baby in a small white box. My brother Charlie and his wife Bobby lost their first child, a son, at birth. He smothered in the birth canal because he weighed 13 lbs. I remember going to Bobby's mother's house where the wake was held. The small box was a white casket in the corner of the living room by a window. The soft breeze was blowing the lace curtains like angel wings over the little white casket. As I stood there with my mother, I asked her why the baby had booboo's on his head and face. His little face was covered in bruises from the forceps. I don't remember what my mother told me but I do remember being upset because the baby was hurt. I did not know what death meant. I never saw the baby after that and wondered what had happened to him. I comforted my sister-in-law when I saw her crying. I suppose I was given the gift of compassion at a very early age. I was three years old.

My sister Ruth was my surrogate mother those first few years. I remember crying for her to brush my hair and bathe me instead of my mother bathing me. She married Wisner Ritchie when she was 19 and when she was 20, my niece Carolyn was born in August right after my birthday. I officially became an aunt at four years old. I would have been an aunt at three years old had Charlie's baby boy not died.

My parents bought the double next door and my sister Ruth and her husband Wissie moved in on one side while my brother Charlie and his wife Bobby moved in on the other side. I walked across the yard several times a day to see Sis and the baby. Then Bobby had a healthy baby girl Danielle the following February. I have always loved babies and felt so happy to have two babies right next door. I did not understand why I was not allowed to hold the babies. My little nieces and I became playmates as they became old enough. They named me "Putie." I do not know the origin of my nickname.

My brother Earl ran off when he was a senior in high school to marry Laura Camardelle, who was 15 years old. I was almost four years old at the time, but I do remember my family being upset because we did not know where Earl was or what had happened to him for over two weeks. The state troopers and police officers were looking for him as a missing person. My mother thought he was dead until we got a phone call from Laura telling my mother that she and Earl had gotten married and were living with her parents. He was 18 years old. I remember my mother crying and saying, "Thank God he was not murdered!"

My brother George married Sarah Marcella. They would often take me on their dates as would Charlie and Bobby and Earl and Laura. I spent a lot of time with Sis and Wissie. I loved them all very much and I knew that they loved me. My sisters-in-law treated me so special whenever I was with them.

Chapter 2 – My Mama

Mama 1946

Charles S. Taylor

Earl C. Taylor   George A. Taylor

My Siblings

Mama, Earl, Daddy   1938
Me, Carolyn + Sis

Ruth (Sis) Taylor Ritchie

CHAPTER 2
My Mama

§

"Do not be afraid, for I have redeemed you; I have called
you by your name, you are mine. Should you pass through
the sea, I will be with you; or through rivers, they will not
swallow you up. Should you walk through fire, you will
not be scorched and the flames will not burn you. For I am
Yahweh, your God, the Holy One of Israel, your savior."

(*The Jerusalem Bible*, Isaiah 43:1-3)

For clarification, it is customary to call one's mother "Mama" and
one's father "Daddy" in the South especially in south Louisiana.

My mama had nicknamed me Betty because she did not want anyone to
call me Lizzie. She registered me in school as Elizabeth Jeannette Taylor,
but when my name was called for report cards or other business, I did not
answer because I thought my name was Betty. When I asked why I had two
names, I was given the Lizzie reason. I wanted to be called Elizabeth, not
Betty. When I graduated from high school, I declared that my name was
Elizabeth. It got shortened to Liz, but some members of my family and
some of my classmates still called me Betty. Betty did not fit me.

I was ready for Kindergarten at five. I wanted so much to learn to
read and write and do numbers. My sister walked me a block away from
home to Our Lady of Prompt Succor School. From the first minute in

Kindergarten, I loved school. My teacher was Miss Clara, who told us that we would be learning to spell, read, write and do math. I was so happy to be in school. When my sister came to pick me up I asked her why so many kids were crying in school. She said they probably missed their mothers. I did not understand why anybody would be crying in this wonderful place where we could learn readin', writin', and 'rithmetic! I loved school and still do!

The very first day of Kindergarten the Pastor visited our classroom. He reminded the class that everyone must attend Mass on Sundays. I do not recall ever going to Mass. When I came home from school, I told my mother that I had to go to church on Sunday because "Father said" I did. I reminded her on Sunday morning. In front of our house was a major street to cross in order to walk a block down to church, so my mother crossed me over and I walked to church by myself. I felt like a big girl. We lined up by class and walked into the church. I watched carefully as everyone sat, kneeled, and stood. My teacher had told us about Communion – that the Host was really Jesus. She had told us stories of the God-Man. I wanted to know more about this Jesus. I watched as people went up to Communion and wondered how Jesus could fit in that little round wafer. I wanted Jesus, too, and did not understand why I had to wait until I was seven to make my First Communion as I was told. After all, I had walked to church all by myself.

The church bells would ring when Mass was over and my mother would be waiting for me so that I could cross the street safely. She did this every Sunday until I was old enough to cross by myself, about age nine. I wondered why she would not go to church with me. She did come when I made my First Communion at seven and again when I made what was called my "Big Communion" and Confirmation at age eleven. Those were the only times she attended Mass until after my father died when I was nineteen.

My mother enrolled me in dance class and piano lessons when I was seven years old. We had dance and music revues every June. My dance teacher Mrs. Tisdale would give me the sketches for the costumes and the material samples to have the costumes made. My mother would give me the money and send me to the store to buy what I needed. Then she would tell me to take everything to the dressmaker a few blocks away. Sometimes the local "dry goods store" as it was called then did not have what I needed, so my mother and I would get on a bus, take a ferry across the Mississippi, take another bus, then a street car to get to downtown New Orleans. Shopping was always fun in the big city. Those were happy times for me.

My mother and I often went to downtown New Orleans. I remember having lunch at the Woolworth's Dime Store. It was so much fun to see all the big stores with so many beautiful things. The store windows had beautiful displays. We would walk for many blocks. Then on the way home we would always stop at the "Big" A & P Grocery Store in Gretna after we had crossed by ferry again. We could not buy a lot since we had to carry the bags of groceries on the bus. We also had to get home before my Dad got home. We had to change clothes and pretend that we had been home all day. He would have gotten angry had he known we had gone to New Orleans. I never understood why. I would have to lie when he questioned me about what we had done that day. I confessed my lie in confession, but failed to say that if I had not lied, my mother would have paid the price. I had a lot of conflict about what I was taught to do in re-ligion classes and what I was told to do by my mother in order to protect her. Till this day I cannot stand to be lied to.

After my confirmation I began attending daily Mass at 6:30 a.m. I am sure I was drawn to the Eucharist by the grace of the Sacrament of Confirmation. Grace kept me going and seeking to know Jesus in a deeper way.

When I was seven years old, I saved my mother's life. Whenever my father was late in getting home, that meant he was out drinking. My mother would always get into my bed. I did not understand why until after I was married. He probably wanted sex and by getting in bed with me she was not available to him. Well, this particular night I woke up to the bed shaking and my mother gasping for air. My father had his knee in her stomach and was strangling her. I can still see that seven year old standing up in her little flannel nightgown with pink rosebuds and ruffles on it. I was screaming as loudly as I could. Fortunately, my brother George and his wife Sarah were living with us temporarily, so George came running into the bedroom with a shotgun. My father locked himself in the bathroom. My sister, who lived next door, heard my screams and came running to the house. She took me home with her. I do not know what happened after that. I do remember that Dr. Gelpi came to the house the next morning to check my mother. Her throat was black and blue and she could not talk. He said to her, "A few more seconds and you would have died." I believe that's when my "Messiah Complex" took over. I had saved my mother before but now when I heard the doctor's words, I realized, even at seven, that I had to protect my mother somehow. I had no knowledge of a Messiah Complex at that age. I was in my 30's before I came to know the meaning and realized that the term applied it to me. This was a battle I have had to fight for a long time. It helps when I say to myself, "Get off the cross, Liz, we need the wood." I don't know where I got this saying. It is a reminder that I am not a savior. There is but one Savior!

When my mother was angry with my father's drunkenness, she blamed me for being born. I felt even more responsible for my mother's well-being when she yelled at me and told me that I should never have been born because now she was forced to stay with my father because of me. I was eight years old at the time. On one occasion she pointed to the bedroom window and told me that she should have thrown me out of that window the day I was born because then she could have left my father. I felt responsible for my mother's pain and did whatever I could to please both of my parents. I became a people-pleaser and a peace-maker at an early age. I believed that there was something really wrong with me. Subconsciously I set out to prove that I belonged here, so I did my best to excel at everything I did. It became my job to make up for my very dys-functional family. Yet, I continued to struggle with feelings of not being good enough, smart enough, pretty enough, and simply enough! I battled feelings of inadequacy a great deal of my life! No wonder I had such a sense of shame about who I was!

I was probably in fifth grade at Our Lady of Prompt Succor Catholic School when I realized that my mother was breaking a Commandment. You see, my mother was a fortune teller and a faith healer. I did not realize that what she was doing was wrong until we studied the Commandments. I remember marching home to tell her she had to stop sinning. I was ten years old. She told me in anger to mind my own business. I kept telling her that what she was doing was wrong, but she kept getting angry at me so I finally stopped. I had so much shame about what she was doing. I was also terrified that the Nuns would find out about it and would no longer love me and let me spend time with them. I sweated every time that Commandment came up in Religion Class the rest of my time at Prompt Succor. I was afraid one of my classmates would tell my teachers that my mother practiced those things. (The Nuns already knew about my mother, so I wasted my energy worrying! They loved me anyway!) My mother would pray over people and sometimes there would be a healing. Other times I would overhear her tell someone what to take to have an abortion. The mixed messages made it harder for me to understand her. I was terrified that she would go to jail and I would be left with my drunken father.

Mama told me the story about how my Daddy would treat everyone to drinks in a bar on payday. He would then come home with little money but with his gut filled with liquor. When she had the first four children, she worried about how she would feed them. That is when she started telling fortunes and healing people. My brothers dropped out of school to earn money by working at a service station. My sister also dropped out of school and went to work at the Five and Dime across the street. My siblings had it a lot harder than I did.

I was about seven years old when Mama took me to visit an elderly lady who was bedridden. I was in class with her granddaughter. The lady had terrible bedsores. I had never seen anything so awful before. I watched as my mother lovingly and gently bathed this lady and put some kind of salve (as they often called medicine) on each of the horrible bedsores. It was very confusing to me. I kept getting double messages from both parents.

I remembered the story of how my mother wanted to be a nurse, but my grandmother told her that no daughter of hers would be emptying bedpans and bathing men. My memories of my grandmother are that of a cynical, critical, mean woman. It is ironic that my grandmother chose to come to our house when she was dying instead of going to my mother's half-sister who lived next door to my grandmother. I was 16 years old at the time and do remember my mother taking excellent care of her own mother. My Mama did have a very compassionate heart.

The story my mother told me about her biological father was that he worked on a banana boat to South America and died of yellow fever on one of his trips right before she was born. The story my sister told me was that my grandmother was a Nanny to a wealthy family in Donaldsonville, Louisiana, and was raped by the man of the house and became pregnant with my mother. My grandmother married the grandfather I knew many years later and had my Aunt Lula. I remember my step-grandfather as a very loving and kind man. He died when I was 17.

So, I know my mother was wounded. She finished 5th grade and went to work in a shrimp factory where she peeled shrimp for eight to ten hours a day. When she was 13, she became a Nanny for the Mayor and his wife in Westwego. She was their children's Nanny until she married at 16. I was named after the Mayor's wife. The people who knew my mother loved her. She was kind and loving to everyone. I realized in later years that her cruel words to me were because she was so wounded and hurting. As they say, "Hurting people hurt people."

She became a different person when she was abused by my father. I was nine years old when she showed me her well- endowed breasts. There were several inch -wide scars on both breasts where the doctor had lanced her breasts to allow the infection to drain out. All she was given to numb the pain was a shot of whiskey. She told me how she sat on a kitchen chair and held a dishpan under her breasts to catch all the infection coming out. I was horrified, especially when she told me the story of how her breasts became infected after my father had dragged her to bed by her breasts, once she had finished nursing my brother Earl. I was really traumatized by the sight of her scars and by her story. I had difficulty understanding how my daddy could do such a horrible thing. My mother confided too much in me at an early age. Some things were beyond my years. I had to grow up fast. I was in a sense the parent to parents who were wounded children. The problem was that I was wounded, too, in the process.

My mother would take calls for a Mr. Muller, who sold some kind of tonic and was also in the car business. I never really understood that situation. She would clean the house, cook a big meal, and Mr. Muller would come over once a week. They closed the door to the dining room while they talked. My mother was always happy when he came. He was always dressed in a nice suit and drove a spotless green Studebaker with whitewall tires. He was very nice to me.

I remember my mother making a nine church walking novena in N.O. where she dragged me along. I was about eight. The purpose of the novena was to pray for my daddy to die so that she could marry Mr. Muller and we could then live in a big house facing Audubon Park. It was so confusing to me. I knew it was wrong to pray for someone to die. I had no one to talk to about this. I was afraid to share this information with my best friend Julie and her mother who was also a surrogate mother to me. I kept everything deep inside. It is a wonder that I turned out to be somewhat sane. Again God's grace was working in me. I have no doubt that I was protected under the wings of His angels.

I don't believe that my mother was having a physical affair with Mr. Muller but she certainly was having an emotional affair. She was in love with him for more than 50 years until the day she died. Yet I watched her lovingly care for my daddy when he was dying for 6 months. Just more confusion and more double messages!

One of the scariest things about going to downtown N.O. was when we went to the French Quarter to visit fortune tellers. I remember sitting in a courtyard all by myself while my mother visited with a strange looking little man who would tell her fortune. I also remember the times we went to a tea room where a lady dressed in what I thought was a costume (I think she was a gypsy) would read tea leaves. I was parked in a chair across the room so I could not hear what was being said. I was between five and nine years old. When I turned ten, my mother would leave me at home or go during school hours. She was convinced that she would one day marry Mr. Muller. I was always confused by what I saw and what I heard. I was also told to keep these things a secret. I had to keep secrets for both parents. It was a real burden for me. I strongly dislike secrets to this day.

I was not free to fix myself a snack when I would come home from school because there would be people sitting in the kitchen waiting their turn to see my mother. There were people from all walks of life. Some of them were there to have their fortunes told and others came for healing. I was always embarrassed so I spent a lot of time in my room.

My mother took me with her to visit a sick friend when I was 11 years old. It was a very hot August day. We walked about seven blocks from the bus to this lady's house. I was very thirsty when we got there and asked for water. The lady took a glass out of the dish drainer and gave me water from the faucet. I noticed that the lady was yellow and looked awfully sick. My mother prayed over her and we left. Three weeks later I started turning yellow. My mother continued to send me to school. She said I had only a very bad cold. The Nuns finally said that I needed to stay home. I was feeling awful. My Sis came over, took one look at me, and called her doctor to come to the house. That is when he diagnosed me with "Yellow Jaundice" as Hepatitis was called in those days. The lady we visited had hepatitis "A" and shared it with us. My mother also came down with it, as well as a friend of mine. I had exposed everyone in my class to the disease. Mama did not believe in doctors. I am grateful that my Sis did not have the same belief.

I was not taught to brush my teeth at home and I never had dental check-ups. I learned to brush my teeth at school in Health Class. So when I got a terrible toothache right before our Mayfair at school, my mother gave me money and sent me to a dentist in Gretna since that was the closest dentist. The man did nothing to save my molar so he pulled it. The next day I danced in the Mayfair at school even though I was in pain. I had learned at an early age to dismiss my pain and keep going. My best friend Julie was again there with me. I would have been afraid to go alone. I never liked going to new places by myself when I was growing up but was forced to at times. I was 12 years old at the time.

I remember having a terrible earache the summer before my sophomore year at Mt. Carmel. My mother washed my ear out with vinegar. My ear became worse, so she gave me money and sent me four towns away to an ear specialist in Algiers. My best friend Julie came with me. I had just turned 15 and, other than the doctor who came to the house when I had Hepatitis "A," I had never been to a doctor. The ear specialist lanced my ear as I cried in terrible pain. He told me not to be such a baby. Besides the abscessed tooth, it was the most painful experience of my life thus far. It seems that I kept getting the message that I was not to show my pain.

When I was 16 years ago, I got a terrible stomachache at boarding school. The Nuns said I had to see a doctor before I could come back to school that Monday. So, when I came home on Friday, I told my mother what the Nuns said and she told me that all I needed was a good dose of castor oil. Thank God I had enough sense to know that with a stomachache, castor oil is not the thing to do. So I asked Julie's Mom to take me to her doctor on Saturday. My mother was not happy about that but gave me the money to pay the doctor bill. The next day I was in the hospital and on Monday had an appendectomy. I am so grateful that the Holy Spirit was guiding me. I had learned to listen to that still, small, inner voice. My angels did overtime in protecting me from harm. It was daily Mass and my relationship with my Lord that helped me through each experience. I am so grateful that He called me by name!

What I learned from these experiences of my mother denying that anything was wrong was not to pay attention to my body. I admit that there were times when I ignored my body until it would not let me ignore it any longer. Sometimes we ignore God and have to learn the hard way.

I have learned with His help to pay attention to my body and the Spirit within for which I am so grateful!

My mother did take me shopping as I outgrew my clothes. Those were fun times with her. She did not limit the clothes I wanted. Thank God I learned to be frugal at an early age. Perhaps this was her way of making up for the harsh times. I had all the material things I wanted and needed, but that did not make up for what I really needed – a safe and secure home with loving parents. I know my parents loved me as well as they could, but they were limited by their own woundedness. I am grateful for what they did give me, especially my Catholic education.

Chapter 3 - My Daddy

Daddy & Me

CHAPTER 3
My Daddy

§

"Do not let your hearts be troubled. Trust in God still, and trust in me. There are many rooms in my Father's house; if there were not, I should have told you, and after I have gone and prepared you a place, I shall return to take you with me; so that where I am you may be too. You know the way to the place where I am going."

(THE JERUSALEM BIBLE, JOHN 14:1-4)

MY FATHER BEGAN WORKING ON the Texas and Pacific Railroad at the age of ten when he had completed fifth grade. He worked his way up to Foreman on the trains. He was a railroad man until he became ill at 68. He rarely took a day off. I remember his taking a vacation every seven years to paint our house. He worked seven days a week, even holidays. I suppose I got my work ethic from him.

His father had died of pneumonia at age 41 and left a pregnant wife with seven young children. Grandpa Taylor was an overseer on a plantation in St. Francisville, Louisiana. With his death my Grandmother had to leave the plantation. She and her children settled in Westwego, Louisiana, across the river from New Orleans. Having to feed so many mouths was a big challenge for her, but since she baked "the best biscuits, pies, and cakes this side of the Mississippi," that is just what she did to support her family. The older boys, including my father, went to work. My father became an alcoholic at an early age as he followed his older brothers' example. His alcoholism was a serious problem in our family. He was 26 years old when he married my 16 year old mother. Their marriage was rocky from the start.

I have had to overcome the shame I had carried for so many years - shame from my parents. It was so humiliating when the neighbors across the street from our driveway would see my Dad come staggering home. I always wanted to hide, but I had to be on guard to protect my mother. When I look back on my childhood, I am amazed at the courage I had to stand up to my father. It had to be God's grace giving me the courage I needed. Fortunately my Daddy never once hurt me physically. The emotional wounds were deep enough. My Dad was hard-working. He never missed work though he had a hangover many a day. He was up at 5:00 a.m. every morning regardless of how he felt, even when he had a cold.

When I was almost six years old, my front baby teeth had not yet gotten loose and the second teeth were coming out behind them. My Daddy took me to the dentist in Gretna to have my baby teeth pulled. It was a most embarrassing moment for me when the dentist pointed down and told me to spit after he had pulled my front teeth. I thought he was pointing to the floor, so being an obedient little girl I spit on the floor. The dentist said, "No, spit in that white bowl!" I did not know what that white bowl was for since I had never been to the dentist before. I felt a lot of shame because I thought I had done something wrong. My Daddy voiced his concern that I would have crooked teeth since the second teeth were out of line. The dentist told him to remind me daily to push the teeth forward with my tongue. I did as I was told and ended up with very straight front teeth. I remember clinging to my Daddy's hand as we walked to the bus to go home. He was a comfort to me then.

I remember helping my Daddy whitewash our picket fence when I was about six years old. That was probably my first experience at painting anything. I loved having a paint brush in my hands. I also remember sitting on his lap while he was drinking beer with a buddy. He forced me to take a sip of beer and the beer came out of my nose as I choked on it. I was about six years old. I probably made the decision never to drink beer or any alcoholic beverages at that time. It was a terrifying and painful experience for me and yet a grace!

I was about six years old when my Dad came home before my mother. A neighbor teen-age girl was my babysitter. I don't remember where my mother was because she had always made it a point to be home when my Dad got home. I remember my Dad standing in the bathroom door motioning to my sitter to come to him. He closed the door behind them and when my sitter came out of the bathroom, she told me that my Daddy was a "dirty old man." I was not sure of what that meant, but I somehow felt shame. He did not appear to be drunk. I was confused!

I was playing in the backyard one evening when I was around ten years old when a neighbor lady asked me to call my daddy out. They went between the houses for a while. I was not sure what that was about, but I remembered my mother telling me that she suspected that my daddy was sleeping with this lady. I don't think I understood what she meant.

I dreaded holidays, especially Christmas. I loved celebrating Jesus' birth but was always anxious about what would happen when my daddy got home. He would always come home drunk on Christmas Day. I remember one Christmas when he dumped the pots on the floor and yanked the tablecloth so that the dishes went flying to the floor. My mother just stood there crying as I yelled at my father to stop. He would then take a nap and wake up not remembering what he had done. My mother would tell him what had happened and he would hang his head as he sat in the rocker in the corner of the kitchen. I would then see a very broken man, yet not broken enough to change his ways. The last Christmas he was with us was very quiet since he was dying of prostate cancer and heart disease. I was 19 years old. It took several years for me to get over being anxious at Christmas.

When my father was sober, he sat with me at night to hear my spelling words, my reading and to help me with my math. Besides academics he appeared to be interested in everything I did in school from plays and school activities to sports, though he never attended any school functions. I was confused by his absence. But when he was drunk, he was mean and violent. I remember standing between him and my mother as he slapped and punched her. I pounded on his stomach with my fists and told him to stop hurting my mama. He could have flung me across the room but he never hurt me physically. He did stop the abuse when I intervened. I was only five years old at the time. I took on the role of trying to fix situations – a role I have carried into adulthood.

My father would wake me up every morning so that I could go to 6:30 a.m. Mass. He came home one evening in a drunken state and accused me of going to Mass to sleep with the priests. I was an innocent young twelve–year-old girl. I was so upset by these accusations. How could he think that of me and of my priests. I later found out that our Pastor was a perpetrator.

At thirteen years old I had gone to play basketball with our team in New Orleans. Our coach was the Assistant Pastor, who drove all nine of us girls to the game. We were packed in his car like sardines. After the game we stopped at an ice cream parlor two blocks from my house to have ice cream. Since we lived close by, my friend and I walked home from the ice cream parlor even though it was 8:00 p.m. Now, my mother had washed and ironed my uniform that very day and I had told her we had a game in N.O. and would not be home until 7 or 8. She was standing in front of our house waiting for me. My friend and I were across the street when I heard my mother yell out, "Where in the hell have you been, girl?" I crossed over and reminded her that I had told her. She could see that I had my basketball uniform on and was with my teammate V. As I got closer to her she yelled, "Your daddy thinks you have been on a lonely road with some man." I was absolutely mortified as I was sure my friend heard her. I was so deeply hurt. My father was already in bed when we went into the house. The next day he said nothing to me. For some reason I did not defend myself. I was feeling a lot of shame, which I later learned was not my shame but my parents' shame. I was being shamed for something I did not do. My father never accused me to my face. He would tell my mother and then she would tell me. It still bothers me when I hear accusations or put-downs second-hand. I am especially very upset when I am accused of something I did not do.

It was around this age that I was awakened one night when my dad sat on the side of my bed. He had been drinking. I sat straight up and he put his arms around my chest and remarked, "My baby has become a woman." I was so terrified that I jumped out of bed and ran into the bathroom until I heard my mother coming out of the living/dining room where she had been telling fortunes with some people. I slept with my softball bat by my bed after that just in case I would need it. My Dad never did anything like that again. I don't know what his intentions were, but I knew that I had to protect myself just in case another incident happened. I never told anyone until I was in therapy in my forties. I was so sad that I could not trust my own father.

I was in eighth grade when my Pastor asked me to play the organ for the children's Masses. As I was practicing one Saturday morning up in the loft of the church, I sensed that someone was behind me. As I turned around, my Pastor planted a very wet kiss on me. I was in shock and said, "Ohhhhhh!" My best friend Julie was doing homework behind the organ. She surprised the Pastor, who did not know she was there, by asking me what was wrong. He then went over to her and kissed her. I turned the organ off and both of us left. I then refused to play the organ again. The Pastor ostracized me from the pulpit, though not by name. He said that there was a certain young lady in the parish who was not willing to share her talents with the church. I knew he was talking about me, but I was too ashamed to tell anyone. Julie and I did tell her mother, who told us never to tell anyone else and to stay away from the Pastor as much as possible. I knew that if I had told my parents, my Dad would make it about me since he had already made terrible accusations. The Nuns did not understand why I would not play the organ. I was too ashamed to tell them.

There was a second incident with my Pastor. A student came to my eighth grade classroom to tell my teacher that the Pastor wanted to see me in the coke room behind the auditorium. I was reluctant to go but didn't know how to explain that to Sr. Alberta. When I went into the coke room, he called me back to a smaller room. I was frightened. He said he just wanted to ask me how I was doing. He said I was turning into a beautiful young woman as he pulled me close to him. I pushed away and told him I had to get back to my classroom to take a test. I lied about the test but I had to get out of there. I was really shaken by that incident. The auditorium was separate from the school. He and I were the only two people there. God again was protecting me! I would not have dared tell my parents about the incident. Oh! The secrets I had to keep!

When I was sixteen, my parents bought me a car – a 1941 maroon Studebaker. I was so excited. We had no car since my mother had given up driving when I was very young. I never knew why. My brother had the Model "A", which I drove when I was 14 and 15. I came home one afternoon and my mother told me to go the bar where my father was treating everyone with his paycheck. Someone had called her to tell her. I was scared to do that, but felt as though I had no choice. I sat outside the bar as I prayed for the courage to walk in to get my drunken father. Two men came out of the bar and asked me what I was doing there. I told them I was there to get my dad but was too afraid to walk into a bar with drunks inside. They asked for my dad's name, which I gave them, then went back inside and brought my dad out. He got in the car with me and I chewed him out all the way home. Again I was feeling so much shame but was also furious that my mother would expect me to get my drunken father out of a bar when I was but 16 years old and also furious at my drunken father. Once again God protected me from harm and gave me the courage I needed to ask for help. Perhaps those two men were angels sent to help me. My God has taken care of me all of my life!

Shortly after that incident I announced to my parents that I would enter the convent when I graduated from Mount Carmel Academy. My Dad came home drunk, grabbed his shotgun and told me he would rather see me dead than in the convent. I ran through the house as he chased me. He fell over a dining room chair and I ran out of the front door. I went to Julie's house for the week-end. When I returned on Sunday afternoon, my

Dad was sitting in the rocker in the kitchen. He appeared to be filled with remorse. God once again poured out His love and grace on me and I said to my father, "It's OK, Daddy, you did not know what you were doing." I am so grateful for the grace of forgiveness. Otherwise I would have grown up very bitter and resentful.

Because I did not believe that I was smart enough to go to College, I enrolled in Soule` Business College after high school graduation from Mount Carmel Academy. My teachers were upset with me for not going to college. After all, I was an honor student and had placed first in the State of Louisiana in English Grammar & Composition. I received a scholarship to LSU but did not use it. The irony of it all is that the gold medal came with Grammar spelled Grammer. I did not send it back to be corrected. It is a conversation piece till this day.

So, I came home after the first week at Soule` and announced that I was not smart enough to learn typing and shorthand. (My high school English teacher Sr. Mary E had told me that any fool can learn typing and shorthand when I announced I would be going to Soule`.) After all, I had had college prep courses in high school and had no idea how to type. I remember saying to myself, "Oh! Where's the 'e' – where's the 'a'?" as I watched the other students typing away since they had had typing in high school. My Dad told me that I could learn to type and do shorthand and that I could not quit. I hung in there and finished a nine-month course in six months. It was a revelation to me that my father thought I was smart. He told me that he really hoped I would become a Pediatrician. Why, I don't know! Three of his father's brothers were country doctors, as was one of his cousins.

Just a few months after I finished business college and was working, my mother woke me up one night in a panic. As I went into their bedroom I could see that my father's lips were blue. I thought he was dead. We got him to the hospital in time. He had had a heart attack. In the course of the examination the doctors discovered that he also had prostate cancer. We were told that it would be a toss-up as to whether he would die from the damaged heart or from the cancer. He was sent home to die! My brothers had a hospital bed put in the living room to make it easier for my mother to care for my father. She slept on the couch next to his bed. My bedroom was next to the living room.

As the cancer spread, I could hear my Dad moaning and groaning all night. It was October of 1953. He was 68 years old. Christmas came and we knew that would be his last Christmas with us. It was also the first Christmas that he was not drunk. I found myself still anxious about the Holidays.

When I came home from work one day in January, my mother told me that my father had something to tell me. I went into the living room where he was now a skeleton of a man. He was 6 feet 1 inch tall and had weighed about 190 lbs. He now weighed about 120 lbs. He grabbed my hand, looked me straight in the eyes and told me that he was going to become a Catholic. I was stunned because we had never discussed the issue. I then asked him why after all these years had he decided to become a Catholic. He said, "Well, I thought if it was good enough for my baby, then it should be good enough for me." That scene still touches me to this day. It was the first time in my life that I realized why God had put me in this family. After all those years of crying myself to sleep on so many nights and asking God why I had been born into this family, I realized that God put me in that family to play a part in my father's salvation and I did not know it until that day. My father was received into the faith and died three months later. For the first time to my knowledge he was in a Catholic church, though in a coffin.

I learned something interesting about my Dad at his wake. There were several black men there. They were standing in a far corner and appeared to be uncomfortable. Segregation was in full bloom at the time. It was 1954. I was never prejudiced – another grace from God – so I walked over to them and thanked them for coming to my father's wake. They worked in the railroad yard and told me that my Dad was always so good to them. They told me how he would give them money for food and medicine when cash was short. They told me what a good man my father was and how sorry they were to see him go. I was deeply touched that these courageous men would come to my father's wake to pay their respects and to share how they knew my father.

I could then focus on the goodness in him and forgive the violent man he became because of the alcohol. God blessed me abundantly that day. I was also blessed by the way my mother lovingly took care of my Dad the six months he was dying. If she could forgive him, certainly I could. God does recycle garbage into grace! St. Ignatius was so right – we can find God in all things.

Eigth Grade Graduation - 13 yrs. old

Kindergarten 5yrs. old

First Grade - 6 yrs old

Fifth Grade - 10 yrs. old

Second grade 7 yrs. old

High School Grad. NCA - 1948 - 19 yrs. old

My School Years

§

"To learn and never be filled is wisdom;
To teach and never be weary is love."

(*APPLES OF GOLD*, COMPILED BY JO PETTY, 1972)

I LOVED SCHOOL. HOMEWORK WAS fun for me. I was like a sponge soaking up all the learning I could. I was always well-behaved so I did everything right to avoid getting into trouble. But I did get into trouble in first grade when the boy behind me kept knocking my books over and sticking my pig tails in the dry ink well in his desk. When I would get up, my hair would pull and it did hurt. Then one day I had had enough of his antics, so I turned around and punched him in the nose. Sr. Agatha was not harsh with me because she knew he deserved it, yet she had to chastise me. It was worth it, though, for he stopped bothering me after that. It helped that Sister moved him to another part of the classroom. (Many years later this boy went to jail.) I excelled, of course, always trying to prove that I was good enough.

The Nuns were so loving and kind to me. School was a happy and safe place to be. I volunteered to help with anything just so I could be with Sisters. I spent hours washing windows and helping in any way I could - my "soul salvation." They showed me God's love and I loved them back. I would practically run down the block to the convent when things were bad at home. I remember sitting on the shiny hardwood floor with my head on Sr. Christina Marie's knee as she stroked my head and comforted me in the old-fashioned "parlor" in the convent. Many times I sought refuge there. My other refuge was Julie and Marmee Verheugen's home. There I was also loved and comforted and made to feel special.

The Sisters recognized something in me so they pushed me to do things I did not think I was capable of doing. I did not think that I could play the piano well enough to play for a school play in eighth grade, but Sr. Alberta said that I could, so with fear and trepidation I did. I was always chosen to be the Blessed Mother in various plays. What an honor it was for me to play Mary!

The Sisters of Mt. Carmel were excellent educators. They were also examples of Christ's love. Sr. Christina Marie was a newly professed Sister when she came to Prompt Succor to teach 2nd grade. I was in 8th grade at the time. We became fast friends then and still are till this day. That was 69 years ago.

I was called "goody-goody two-shoes" by some classmates. I remember a hurtful incident at the school Mass, when instead of my classmates moving down to the end of the pew, they stuck their legs out when I came back from Communion. I had to crawl over their legs to get to the other end of the pew. As I did so, I heard them say "Goody, goody, two-shoes! She thinks she is so holy!" I also got double messages from them. They voted me for many things, yet ostracized me because I attended daily Mass.

When I graduated from 8th grade, I received the highest award given. My daddy came to my graduation and was so excited when my name was announced that he fell off the chair getting up to applaud. I did not expect the award since one of my classmates had told me before the ceremony that she was chosen to receive the award. It was a lovely surprise. In spite of the evidence all around me, I still did not believe that I was smart enough, good enough, or just enough. But if it had not been for the Sisters and for my best friend Julie and her mother Marmee, I have no idea where my life would have taken me. God blessed me with them so I could come to know

Him and see His hand in my life long before I knew Ignatian Spirituality. I have so much to be thankful for!

When it came time to take the entrance exam to Mt. Carmel Academy, Sr. Alberta asked me to not do my best on the exam, since I did not need a scholarship but another classmate did. So, I deliberately put down wrong answers on the Math section. My classmate did get the scholarship. I was afraid I would not be accepted, but I am sure the Nuns caught on. I was ecstatic when I received the call from Mother Angela telling me that I had been accepted.

I had all summer of 1948 to prepare for going to Boarding School at Mt. Carmel Academy. The thought of living with the Sisters was so exhilarating that I could hardly wait until August!

In my freshman year I shared a room with three other girls. The one drawback to boarding school was having to rise at 5:30 a.m. for 6:00 a.m. Mass each morning. However, I was so happy to be there I really did not mind. After school we changed our uniforms, which were brown wool pleated skirts (rather hot when school began), white blouses, a brown Eisenhower wool jacket, brown oxfords and white socks. I was so proud to wear that uniform. I remember having to wear brown culottes for P.E. I made my own, since my mother had sent me to sewing classes at Singer Sewing when I was 13 even though she did not sew. We had to kneel on the floor to be sure that our culottes hit the floor. Of course, we could not have our knees showing!

One day after school I was walking down the hall as the elevator opened. Sr. A came out of the elevator, took one look at me and said, "You should not be wearing that outfit"! I was wearing a straight wool skirt, not tight at all, and a loose-fitting, pullover sweater. I was tall and thin. I asked her why and she said, "Because you might seduce someone!" Puzzled, I looked around and said, "Sister, just whom would I be seducing? There are no boys around here." She was not one of my teachers, but lived at the Motherhouse where the boarding school as well as the Novitiate was. She just told me to go on. Many years later I learned that this Nun had left the convent because she was a lesbian. I did not know what a lesbian was until my late twenties.

Then I realized why we boarders were not allowed to go into each other's rooms!

I became fast friends with Glee DeRouen, now Sr. B (Sr. Mary Bartholomew DeRouen), from the very beginning of my days at Mt. Carmel. We are still close friends after 67 years. Glee was upset with me when I changed my mind about entering the convent with her after we graduated, but she got over it. We had planned to enter the convent together. We did share many good times together. I have not seen her for a few years since I have not been able to travel. She lives in a nursing home in Carencro, Louisiana. She has battled Parkinson's disease for about the past 18 years. It saddens me that a brilliant woman had to give up giving retreats and ministering to so many. I hold her ever in my heart.

The Sisters of Mount Carmel were a very important influence in my life. I doubt that I would be where I am today without their love, encouragement and education. Mother Angela, our Principal, who appeared to be very stern and strict, was very caring. We were not allowed to take the elevator down from the fourth floor, so on Fridays we lugged our books, (no book bags in those days) and our luggage down four flights of stairs. Mother Angela's office was at the foot of the stairs on the first floor. As the boarders were leaving on this particular Friday, I tripped over the suitcase of the person in front of me and went bouncing down the stairs with books flying one way and my suitcase another way. There was Mother Angela standing by her office door watching me. She said to me, "Miss Taylor, that was not very lady-like!" Then she ran to her desk, got the smelling salts and asked me if I was OK as I was sprawled on the floor. She really pushed me to be all that I could be. When I was a junior she came into the classroom to ask volunteers to write an essay on "The Marriage of Figaro" which was coming to the theater in New Orleans. There was a city-wide contest so the winners would receive two tickets to the performance. I did not raise my hand. She called me into the hall and wanted to know why I did not volunteer to write the essay. I told her that I did not think I wrote well enough. She looked at me sternly and said, "You will write that essay, Miss Taylor!" I did and I won! I am so grateful for Mother Angela, Sr. Augusta Marie, Sr. Carmelita, Sr. Mary Edward and Mother Marcella for recognizing gifts that God had given me and pushing me to use those gifts. Furthermore, I knew that they loved me. I certainly loved them.

When I came home on a Friday from school my junior year, my mother said that the Sisters at my grade school had called to ask her permission for me to drive them out to the country three hours away from New Orleans. My mother said that I could, so Mother Elizabeth, Sr. Martina, and Sister Jane Frances headed to Lafayette, Louisiana, on Saturday morning. I was delighted to be spending time with them. I drove them to a small country town near Lafayette to see a priest, who was a relative of Mother Elizabeth. As we headed back to Lafayette that evening, my car lights went off as I drove on a lonely, dirt road on the way to the highway. Sr. Martina sat in the back seat as she prayed the Rosary out loud and asked God to get us to the highway safely. I was not at all nervous or anxious. That's what youth will do for you!!!!! We came upon the only sign of people on a farm out in the boondocks. I pulled into the driveway and went up to the house to ask for help. An old farmer came out. He said he could not help me since he only knew how to work on tractors and trucks. I thanked him and started out again in the unlit country road. Sr. Martina upped the prayers and the pitch of her prayers. I assured her that we would make it safely. I was a fearless 16 year old who really believed what I was saying.

We finally made it to the highway where there was a service station. I breathed a sigh of relief and thanksgiving as I listened to Sr. Martina praising God for getting us to a lit highway. The service station attendant found the problem immediately. He replaced a fuse and lo and behold, my headlights were on again. God really took care of us. We then headed to the convent where we would be spending the night. My fifth grade teacher Sr. Mary William was at the convent and so graciously made sure that I had a meal and whatever else I needed for the night. I was excited about spending the night there. We headed back to New Orleans the next morning. It was a blessing to me that the Sisters trusted me to drive them out of town. Mother Elizabeth also trusted that we would make it through the scary experience of being on a lonely, dark, dirt country road without lights. She trusted God first and then trusted me. The Sisters helped to build my confidence. I loved them so much and was loved by them! A few months later I found myself teaching both Mother Elizabeth and Sister Jane Frances how to drive because the parish was going to buy them a car. That was so much fun!

Being at Mt. Carmel was the best time in my growing up years. I really wanted to enter the convent then. My favorite teacher Sr. Augusta Marie was prefect of the boarders. My room was right next to hers. She encouraged me, comforted me, pushed me and loved me. In my junior year when I decided that I would enter the convent after graduation, she convinced me that I needed to date first, then I could decide with prayer whether or not I had a vocation to the religious life. She was a very wise woman. I had the right motive for entering. I had wanted to serve God in a special way ever since I was a very young child. At the same time I would not consider marriage because of the example of the marriage my parents had. So Glee (Sr. B) got me a blind date to the Jesuit Junior/Senior Prom. We double dated. My date was George Wiltz, who later became a Jesuit. I teased him in later years when he became the Director at the Montserrat Retreat House in Dallas. I said, "George, one date with me and you ran off to the priesthood. I have been ruined for life!" It is amazing how God works! Our paths did not cross for many years until he came to Dallas where we now lived. We reconnected and he ended up inviting me to give retreats at the Retreat House.

Back to dating. Ronnie and I had been best buds all through grade school and high school. We made a pact together that he would become a priest and I would be a nun. After we graduated from 8th grade, he went off to the Benedictine Seminary in Covington, Louisiana. I would visit him with his parents and Julie. We were very close. The summer after our junior year Ronnie told me that he was not going to return to the seminary, that he no longer wanted to be a priest. He said that he was in love with me and wanted to spend his life with me. I talked to Sr. Augusta Marie about it and she believed that I loved Ronnie as well, but had been denying that love. Once again she encouraged me to date. That summer changed my heart. Ronnie was my first love. Our parents were thrilled and were beginning to talk about when we would marry. We also talked about marriage.

Ronnie enrolled in Jesuit High School in New Orleans. Then there was a change of heart that summer after graduation. We began to argue. We broke up and Ronnie soon had another girlfriend. I was crushed about it. At the time I was attending Soule` Business College with the intention of becoming a secretary. I was ready to begin another phase of my life. I wasn't sure where God was leading me. I just kept on stepping out in faith!

Chapter 5 - My Working Career

Loyola University College of
Pharmacy Secretary 1953

CHAPTER 5

My Working Career

§

"I will instruct you, and teach you the way to go;
I will watch over you and be your adviser."

(THE JERUSALEM BIBLE, PSALM 32:8)

AFTER GRADUATION FROM SOULÉ BUSINESS College I began my working career as the Private Secretary to the Dean of Pharmacy at Loyola University in New Orleans. I was 18 years old. My plans were to work five years then travel Europe. I loved my job. There were 123 students in the College of Pharmacy and only three were girls. At exam time I had lots of dates since I typed up the exams. The guys could not get the questions from me though. The Dental School was downstairs in the building. The Dental students had to come up to our floor to get formaldehyde, so I had dates with a few future dentists as well as future pharmacists. It was a fun time in my life. In those days girls dated lots of guys until Mr. Right came along.

One of my Soulé friends was a secretary in another department at Loyola. She asked me if I would be interested in a blind date. My first response was "NO!" She convinced me that this guy was worth it. So I relented and said "Yes!" So, on April 18, 1953, Robert (Bob) Moulin showed up at my front door and swept me off my feet. He was dressed in a light blue sports coat, white shirt, navy tie, navy slacks, white bucks, and sported a crew cut. I was enamored with his appearance and with his smile and with the fact that he would drive 30+ miles to pick me up. Then we drove back to New Orleans to attend the Icecapades with Pat & Eddie. Then he had to bring me home and turn around and drive back to New Orleans himself. I liked him from the start and was looking forward to our next date. Well, he did not call me for a whole month. When he finally called, I had dates to the Loyola University Dental School Dance, the Pharmacy School Dance, and a couple of other dances. It was the end of the semester and also graduation time. He finally said, "Well, when are you free for a date?" I gave him a day and time and he showed up. He showed up every night after that. I had to cancel my dates with the other guys. I was just 18 but somehow knew he was the one.

Just a few months later I had a job opportunity at Avondale Marine Ways. I was making $175.00 per month at Loyola Univ. and this job would pay me $300.00 per month. I was sorry to leave the Pharmacy School, but besides the salary being great at the time, Avondale was just 15 minutes from my house. I jumped at the chance since my relationship with Bob was getting serious. In October of that year was when my father became ill. Bob was a great support to me.

Working for the Credit Manager at Avondale was quite a challenge for an 18 year old. He was a perfectionist, who would allow for no mistakes. Part of my job was typing 7 copies each of invoices for the Navy (Avondale had Navy contracts) and barges, etc. for large shipping corporations. I had to have the invoices on his desk by 4:30 p.m. when he would take a magnifying glass and go over each one to see if I had made any mistakes. In those days we had only erasers to correct mistakes and those were taboo. Besides, how could an original and 6 carbon copies withstand erasing!

I was at Avondale about three months when Mr. S bought me a new typewriter. I typed about 36 invoices that day plus correspondence and placed everything on his desk by 4:30 p.m. He was constantly telling me how great his former secretary was and how she had set a record of getting the most invoices out. Well, I set a record that day. I always rise to a challenge, but not without tension. He threw the first three invoices on my desk and said to me, "Miss Taylor, you have made a mistake on every one of the 8's on these invoices. You will have to stay and redo them. I was furious! I put a piece of paper in my new typewriter and typed 8's across the page. It seems that the new Royal typewriter had a backward apostrophe attached to the top of the 8's whereas the old Underwood had perfectly round 8's. I threw the newly typed page of 8's on his desk and said, "Then throw this typewriter out!" and ran off to the restroom to cry. I dried my tears and went back to the office. I was sure I would be fired. Mr. S had put all of the invoices back on my desk to be folded and made ready to mail. He said not a word to me. I was waiting for an apology but, of course, never received one.

I also did the accounts receivable every week. I had to balance the books, type up a report and have it on the VP's desk by 3 p.m. every Friday. This particular Friday I could not balance the books. Consequently, the VP did not get his report. Mr. S was very upset with me. Again I was sure I would get fired. After work I asked Bob to meet me in the park. I was so afraid to get fired. I told him what happened and he reassured me that I would find the problem when I went into work on Saturday. I dried my tears and was determined to balance those books the next day. Bob has always been so supportive of me.

I didn't sleep Friday night. I prayed a lot! I could not stand to think that I was in trouble. So, I went into the office early Saturday morning and was determined to get the job done. We had lots of payments that had to be posted in three places. We are talking about thousands of dollars and many checks. Well, lo and behold, Mr. S had received a payment from one of our accounts and had posted it in only one place. I wanted to jump up and down and scream to the mountain tops. I showed Mr. S his mistake and all he said was, "Now, you can get that report to the VP!" Again, there was no apology for his rudeness to me on Friday afternoon. I continued to work for him for two years until I was expecting my first baby. Bob and I had married the year before. After I left and had Tara, Mr. S called me to ask me to come back to work for him. Of course, I declined but could not help but smile. He ended up hiring two people to take my job. Because I had worked extra hard to prove that I was good enough, it seems that I had set the bar very high. Yet, it would be many years before I could really own that I was good enough!

So, what did I learn in the two years at Avondale? I learned to be a fast and perfect typist. I learned bookkeeping, which in later years allowed me to do my own books for my business. I learned that even though someone does not apologize for hurting me does not mean that I cannot forgive the person. I learned to rise to the challenge and to persevere in whatever I do. There again, I can understand the Ignatian way of finding God in all things! I also learned about office politics and that I did not care to work in an office again!

Chapter 6 - Marriage & Children

Wedding Day - 7-19-54 Bob + Liz

Marriage & Children

§

"Ask, and it will be given to you; search, and you will
find; knock, and the door will be opened to you...
If you, then, who are evil, know how to give your
children what is good, how much more will your
Father give good things to those who ask Him!"

(*THE JERUSALEM BIBLE*, MATT 7:7-11)

I HAVE ALREADY WRITTEN ABOUT my blind date with Bob and how he did
not call me for a month for a second date. I thought he did not like me until he called and was persistent about going out with me again. From that
second date on he drove over to see me every night. On Saturday nights
we would drive back to New Orleans to see a movie, after which we would
go to the Café du Monde for coffee and beignets. We would talk for a couple of hours, then head back to Westwego. On the way to my house was
a restaurant called "The Flying Saucer." That was our final stop for the
best hamburgers and the very best chocolate pie from Gambino's Bakery,
my favorite. The other six nights of the week we spent in my living room,
often with my Grandpa Sourita, who would come over to watch TV with
us. My parents bought a TV in 1948 when TV's first became the "thing
to have." I was always glad that my Grandpa went home early so that Bob
and I could be alone.

Bob's mother would ask him, "Who is your date tonight?" He would tell it was Elizabeth Taylor. Her comment was always, "Well, if you don't want to tell me, I will let it go!" But she never did until I met her sister Aunt Julie three months later. Aunt Julie told his mother that that was my real name. After we had been dating for four months I was invited to Bob's house for Sunday dinner. I remember being so nervous about using the right fork and following etiquette that I woke up with a migraine that morning. The dining room where we were to eat had windows all across. I was told where to sit. My chair was facing the bright sunshine coming in through the windows. I was squinting before we sat down, so Bob offered to change places with me because the bright sunlight was hurting my eyes. His mother returned from the kitchen, placed her hands on the back of her chair and very calmly said, "The guest always sits to the right of the host!" I was now to the left of Bob's father. I felt so humiliated. Bob came to my rescue by telling his mother that he changed places with me because the sunlight was bothering me since I had a migraine. She said nothing. I thought she would understand since she suffered from migraines as well. I was almost in tears and kept telling myself that I had blown it. At the same time I admired Bob for standing up to his mother by taking care of me. I was concerned that she would not approve of me. That turned out to be true!

Our next meeting was a Saturday when I went over to pick up Bob since his parents would be using their car. Mrs. Moulin was giving an art lesson, so I said a quick "Hello" and we were off to a Tulane/LSU game that October afternoon. Bob later told me that his mother told him that I had nice legs. I was surprised that she had complimented me to him.

Thanksgiving and Bob's birthday coincided that November. Since my mother was spending time in the hospital with my dad, who had had a heart attack, there would be no Thanksgiving dinner at our house. Bob mentioned my coming to his house for dinner. I don't know what happened but I suspected that Mrs. Moulin did not like the idea. She and Bob had a big argument. He called to tell me that he and I would be eating dinner at a restaurant. We ended up at my favorite restaurant. In our conversation Bob began talking about "when we get married" etc. He did not officially propose but it sure sounded as though he had made up his mind that I was the one. We had been dating steadily since May. I was thrilled but also had some fear and trepidation about how his mother would react to the possibility that he would marry me. We continued to talk marriage but did not mention it to anyone else.

I had to have a pilonidal cyst removed from my spine in March. My father was dying so my mother could not be with me. Bob came to the hospital to be with me. His tender loving care convinced me even more that he was the one. I was given a spinal for the surgery and ended up with severe headaches and dizziness for several weeks. I went right to bed when I came home from my job at Avondale my first day back on the job. Bob came over a little while later. My mother told him I was lying down because I had "one of those headaches." She told him to go back to my bedroom. He sat on the side of the bed and said that he had something that would make me feel better. Then he slipped a ring on my finger. It was quite a surprise. I flew out of bed, headache and all and ran in to show my parents. My dad was very weak but very lucid. He grabbed Bob's hand, kissed it and said, "Now I can go because I know my baby will be taken care of!" It was a wonderful glimpse of loving behavior from him. My Daddy died 20 days later on April 29, 1954. We had planned a September wedding originally but moved it up to July because we thought my dad would survive until then. He told me before he died that he did not want me to change my wedding plans should he die before then. He wanted me to get married in July. We honored his wishes. I was so sad that he could not be at our wedding.

For several months we had stopped at a jewelry store window to admire the rings on our walk to the movie theater. I would point to a set and tell Bob how beautiful the rings were. One Saturday night the rings were not in the window. I was crushed because I thought someone had bought my beautiful rings. Bob kept a straight face for three months. I had no clue that he had put the rings in lay-a-way. When he paid them off, we became engaged.

The next three months were a whirlwind planning the wedding. First we had to get through my daddy's funeral. I asked my dearest friend Julia to be my Maid of Honor and another dear friend V to be my Matron of Honor. My mother and I went shopping for my wedding dress and found one at the first store we went into. The dress fit perfectly and was delivered the day before my bridal portraits were scheduled. Much to my dismay, there was a huge coke or coffee stain on the train of the gown. I was crushed. Tears began to flow. It was just two weeks before my wedding day. I was so distressed. My mother scolded me for being distressed. I did not know that a surprise bridal shower was scheduled for that evening. I suppose she did not want me to attend with swollen and red eyes. I managed to stop crying and re-grouped. Julia and I were planning to go to another friend's shower that evening, so I was to pick her up at Aunt Mamie's. As I walked in the back door of Aunt Mamie's house, I heard, "Surprise!" It was my bridal shower. I am not easily surprised but this time they got me. It was a lovely shower that eased my distress over my stained bridal gown.

I did get the bridal portraits done since the photographer assured me that the stain would not show. My mother, Julia and I then headed downtown to take the gown back and hopefully get another one. The store had another one in a larger size. The alternative was to have the gown altered or to start the search for another gown. I could not chance finding another gown in such a short time so I chose to have it altered. I would get it just a few days before the wedding day. I prayed that it would fit and not have any stains. Fortunately, it arrived without stains and with a perfect fit. God hears prayers for simple things like wedding dresses!

Bob and I were going to live in Aunt Regina's upstairs apartment, so the week before the wedding was spent packing up and moving as much as we could. My brother George and Sarah helped us move. George hoisted my bed over the balcony of the apartment since it would be too difficult to go up the stairs with it. Our apartment consisted of one bedroom, a bath and a kitchen. We were so excited about our first home together.

On a very hot July 19th, 1954, I became Mrs. Robert John Moulin at Our Lady of Prompt Succor Church. We had a lovely reception afterwards. There was some sadness that my daddy could not be there, yet I knew that he was looking down from Heaven. I was comforted by that thought. I gave thanks to God for His many blessings on me – my wonderful husband, my daddy's conversion and peaceful death, and my mother's return to the Church. I was one very happy bride!

We spent our honeymoon in Biloxi, Mississippi. One of the things we did was go to Ships Island on a boat that probably held about 30 people. The Gulf was very rough that day. I spent that evening dealing with my first bout of seasickness. Fortunately I recovered overnight. We returned to New Orleans to our little, cozy apartment. We spent the week-end moving the rest of my things and Bob's things so we could be settled in before both of us returned to work on Monday.

My boss was not happy when I called in two days later to tell him I was ill. I had fever and ached all over. I had picked up some kind of bug that kept me home until the following Monday. I was concerned about what the office staff would think. Of course, I was teased when I returned to work. My co-workers insisted that I had stayed home to extend our honeymoon. I reminded them that a honeymoon of one, especially one who was sick, was really not a honeymoon. Bob had his second experience in being my nurse and caretaker. I was well taken care of. I was very upset that I had gotten ill. I am the giver, so receiving was always hard for me. I have been given multiple opportunities to receive over the years. God always knows what we need!

We settled into married life quite well. I thanked God daily for His many blessings, especially for Bob, the love of my life. We were attending Midnight Mass when I became very nauseated. I thought I was coming down with a virus or the flu. I began throwing up the day after Christmas. It did not stop for over 24 hours. I managed to get a doctor's appointment the next day. Dr. Larry McCune said that I might be pregnant but it was too soon to tell. There were no pregnancy tests in those days. He gave me a shot for the nausea and miraculously I stopped throwing up until the next Sunday then started all over again for 24 hours. I was back in his office on Monday morning for another shot. This scene continued for several weeks. When Larry told me I was pregnant, I said, "Wow! I was so afraid that I would not be able to get pregnant!" He asked how long we had been married. I said, "Five months!" He started laughing and told me he would have been concerned if I had said five years, but certainly not five months. We were thrilled about becoming parents the following August.

In the meantime Bob's mother bought a duplex. We were going to need more room so the plan was for us to rent the downstairs. We would have three bedrooms, two baths, a large living room/dining room combination, a hallway large enough for a washer and eventually a dryer and a fenced- in yard. The duplex was right across the street from the Sugar Bowl Stadium on the Tulane University Campus. We were so excited about having a nursery to decorate. Moving day would be the end of September.

We were cleaning and preparing the duplex when Bob's cousin came over to see the place. She took one look at me and told me I was ready to deliver. I wasn't due for another 6 days. Lo and Behold! She was right! The very next morning I woke up with irregular labor pains. Bob stayed home that day just in case. We called Larry McCune, who said it sounded like false labor but if the pains became regular then we should head to the hospital. That happened about 4 p.m., so off we went to Mercy Hospital. I was there less than two hours when we welcomed Tara Jeanne Moulin into the world on August 17, 1955. I was out when she was born so I did not know the sex of the baby. There were no Sonograms in those days. I woke up to Bob telling someone on the phone that the nurses said "she is the prettiest baby ever born at Mercy Hospital!" I then knew we had a girl. In those days the mother was the only one who got to hold the baby once every three hours. Bob did not get to hold Tara until four days later when we were preparing to go home. I am glad that this policy has changed. Babies need to be held by their Daddies from the very beginning of their lives. Tara was my 21st birthday present.

Our first night at home Tara cried the entire night. It was terribly hot and all we had was a fan – no A/C. So the windows were open. I am sure we kept the whole neighborhood awake. Bob took over her care that first week. The second day I wanted to bathe her and change her but he wanted to take care of her. Then I realized that I would have her all to myself after that week when he was back at work. I graciously let him bond with his daughter. He did diaper duty, walked her for hours every night, fixed meals, etc. He was and is a Super Dad. Everyone was amazed at how he just took over since he had not been around babies. Bob was an only child.

I remember how we both sat on the side of the bed and stared at our beautiful daughter. We marveled at God's handiwork. She was so perfect in every way. We gave thanks for her every day and we still do! God had truly blessed us beyond our dreams! What a miracle a baby is!!!!!!

My Mother came to help me the second week. She slept downstairs in Aunt Regina's house. She was a big help as she cooked and cleaned. Aunt Regina let us use her washer for the diapers and laundry. She had no dryer so the clothes were hung outdoors. I was not allowed to go up or down the stairs so it was a big help to have my 60 year old mother take care of the laundry and the cooking.

We had planned to christen Tara when she was two weeks old. Bob and my mother met Julie, Tara's Godmother; Eddie Broussard, the Godfather; Bob's mother and father, Cousin Ruth, Aunt Julie and Aunt Regina at Our Lady of Good Counsel Church on Napoleon Avenue for the Baptism. All of them went over to Bob's parents' house afterwards. I didn't know there would be a party. I thought they were coming back to our apartment right after the Baptism. Finally, Bob called me to ask me if I thought I could make it over there if he came to get me. I was feeling very left out so I told him to come for me. I would take my time with the stairs. I had been told not to climb stairs for at least three weeks. I was sorry that I had to miss the Baptism.

Tara was 6 weeks old when we moved to 2529 Calhoun Street. We had set up her nursery, but kept her in the bassinet in our bedroom until she was almost three months old. Again we would sit on the bed and watch her sleep and watch her every move in amazement. She began to sleep 12 hours from 7 p.m. to 7 a.m. every night. We were finally getting to sleep all night. What a gift!

I really enjoyed being a stay-at-home Mom. I made curtains for the windows and had so much fun decorating the house. I enjoyed cooking and trying new recipes! I became quite a "Suzie Homemaker." When the weather was nice, we walked around the neighborhood every day. Life was so good!

Tara was four months old when I discovered I was pregnant again. My second baby would be due at the end of September. Tara would be 13 months old. My morning sickness was not as severe as it had been with my first pregnancy. However, when I was three months pregnant, I was threatening to miscarry. Had to stay in bed for a couple of weeks and get hormone shots. I was finally on my way after that and began to feel great. I loved being pregnant. I had fun making my maternity clothes and little dresses for Tara.

Christopher Michael Moulin was born on September 20, 1956. We were delighted to have a boy. I had had a quick and easy delivery. Surprisingly I managed two babies very well at 22 years old! Chris was a very easy going baby. He did take forever to eat. At the 2:00 a.m. feeding he would smile and coo at me, so the milk would run down his chin. I loved it, but at the same time, I wanted him to get his fill and let me get back to sleep until the next feeding. He, too, started sleeping all night at about 6 weeks old. That was another blessing.

Tara was about 20 months old when she stooped down and screamed in severe pain. I called the Pediatrician and was told to get to the hospital right away. I asked a neighbor to take care of 7 month old Chris and rushed over to the ER. The doctors determined that she would need a lower GI exam. I was not allowed to go into the room with her but stood outside the door as she kept yelling, "Mommy, Mommy, Mommy!" I was so distraught that I could not hold her and comfort her. The diagnosis was an intussusception where the bowel slips down into the adjacent bowel. Surgery is usually required to fix the problem. God once again heard my prayer. The barium enema straightened out the bowel so surgery was not required. It was a terrifying experience for both Tara and me.

I had mentioned to my doctor that I wanted all of my children by the time I was 30 years old. My own experience with an older mother had not been a good one. Bob and I had decided that we wanted 6 children. (My, my, what youth can do to your thinking!) Bob again jumped in with the care of both children. My mother came for about 14 days. She was a big help! She was always available when I had a doctor's appointment. We had a good relationship when I was an adult. God had done a lot of healing in me.

Chris was fascinated with his sister Tara. He watched her intently and followed her around when he began to walk. He would do whatever she told him to do, which got him into trouble at times. When he was 17 months old, I became pregnant with our third child. Since there were no sonograms in those days, we were always surprised when I delivered.

Lisa was born on November 1, 1958. She weighed 6 lbs. 1 oz. and was two weeks early. I had had pneumonia three weeks earlier. When Lisa was two weeks old, I had a severe hemorrhage while at home with a three-year- old, a two- year- old, and my newborn baby. My mother had become ill and was not able to come to my rescue. My mother-in-law was playing bridge, so we had to ask a neighbor to stay with the children while I went to the hospital. Bob had to come home from work to take me. I was going into shock in the ER. My OB Doc worked on me in the ER. Then I was taken to surgery for a D&C. I remember waking up during the night to see my doctor sitting by my bed with his head in his hands. I thought to myself that this must be serious. He later told me that he feared that I would have to have a hysterectomy since the bleeding had been so severe, so he stayed for several hours to watch me. Thanks be to God I did not need further surgery. Dr. Larry McCune was the most caring OB/Gyn. I am so grateful that he delivered all my babies. He did not charge us for the D&C since our insurance would not cover it. We were so grateful since money was scarce in those days!

I came home to recover from pneumonia, a delivery, and a hemorrhage. My Mom was still sick. My sister was taking care of her. I was told not to lift my children and to stay off my feet. Bob could not take any more time off since he had used up his vacation and sick days to stay with me when I had pneumonia and when I had Lisa. My mother-in-law was not the type to help, so I was on my own. One of her young friends came over for the first day only.

I thought the worst was over, not so, not so. About the third day home, Tara and Chris flooded the bathroom by putting the stopper in the sink while Tara was washing her hands. I was busy feeding Lisa when I heard the water running. The sink overflowed and flooded the bathroom. I was not allowed to mop, so I grabbed towels to soak up the water, then changed both children, who had soaked their only pair of high top shoes. The kitchen sink had stopped up the night before and I was waiting on the plumber that day. I threw myself across my bed once I got the kids down for a nap and cried while I told God that I knew I had broad shoulders, but that the past few weeks were more than I could bear. I fell asleep and woke up to a baby crying.

"Life must go on!" I said. I had a baby to feed! So, I slowly crawled out of bed and did what I was called to do! God always supplied the strength I needed to do what I had to do!

The following week three-week- old Lisa developed pneumonia and was very ill. The Pediatrician felt sorry for me, so he did not send us to the hospital. Instead he had us make a tent over the bassinet with a humidifier. The instructions were to watch Lisa's lips and breathing and take her temperature frequently and if her lips turned blue, her breathing became shallow, or her fever went up, we were to get to the hospital immediately. So, Bob fed the children and put them in their cribs with toys. Then went off to the office. I stuck my head under the tent as I watched Lisa's every breath. Bob came home at noon to feed the kids and put them down for a nap. I ate lunch while he watched Lisa. Then he had to go back to the office. When Tara and Chris woke up, they wanted to get up. Tara could climb out of her crib but Chris had not yet learned how to. I had to ask her to play with her brother until Daddy came home. I continued to watch Lisa under the tent while I was deeply concerned about the other two children as well.

Bob came home at 5:30 p.m. I was so happy to see him. He took over watching Lisa while I fixed dinner, fed the kids, played with them, bathed them and got them to bed at 7:00 p.m. Then Bob ate before he took over the "watch" so that I could sleep until midnight. I took over then so that Bob could sleep. Lisa's fever was down in the morning so Dr. Henry Simon said that I did not need to watch her constantly. I was very exhausted and looked forward to naptime for the kids. Lisa recovered and so did I.

Lisa gained very little weight by the first month check-up. We chalked it up to her having had pneumonia. By six months old she weighed only 9 lbs., having gained only 3 lbs. in 6 months. I voiced my concern that something was wrong with her. The doctor did several tests including testing for cystic fibrosis since Lisa had had several bouts of bronchitis. We saw the Pediatricians often. Nothing showed up. By one- year-old Lisa weighed a little over 13 lbs. I kept voicing my concern that there was really something wrong with her.

Lisa came down with yet another case of bronchitis with high fever. It was a Sunday morning when I called the doctor. The Pediatrician who was on call told me I was just a neurotic mother. I told him that my baby was very ill and that I would be glad to meet him in the ER. He reluctantly said he would come to the house. Doctors made house calls in those days. He walked into the house very arrogantly and asked in an exasperated tone where the baby was. I took him back to her room where she was lethargic and her breathing was labored. He gave her a penicillin shot and said to bring her in the next day for another shot. He agreed that she was very ill and probably had pneumonia. He changed his attitude as he left. I told him that when I call and say that my child is sick, she really is. He was not our regular Pediatrician. As President of the Staff at a prominent hospital in New Orleans, I thought he could have used a lesson or two in listening to his patients' parents. We were frequent visitors to the Pediatrician's office for the next several years.

When Lisa was a little over three years old, I became pregnant again. I was threatening to miscarry again at 7 weeks. Again it was bed rest and hormone shots. I made it through this crisis with God's help and began to feel great. Gregory John Moulin was born October 7, 1962. The day I came home from the hospital Tara and Chris brought several classmates home to see their baby brother. I stood in the doorway so they could see him because I did not want him exposed to a lot of germs from about seven kids. Lisa was almost four at the time. I was 28 years old when I had Greg. My OB remembered that I had said I wanted all of my children by the time I was 30 years old. His first words to me after the delivery were, "Well, you have two more years, better get busy. You can have at least two more!!!!!!" If looks could kill, he would have been one dead doctor!!!!!

Greg was about 6 months old when my next-door neighbor rang my doorbell. As I opened the door she was holding four-year-old Lisa, who was screaming. The neighbor's son had knocked Lisa off her swing. When Lisa landed on the concrete below, she put her arm out to catch herself and broke her elbow. Her arm was bent the opposite way. Tara and Chris went over to a neighbor's house while another neighbor drove us to the ER. I had to take Greg with me. The neighbor's sister held Greg while I held Lisa. I called Bob at the office and he met us at the hospital. He turned completely white when he saw Lisa's arm. I was amazingly calm, as I usually am in a crisis, but then stress out afterwards. Lisa's arm had to be set in surgery, which meant a general anesthetic. She had a terrible reaction to the anesthetic, so I had to hold her down in the bed once she was in her room. It was an awful experience for both of us.

The doctor told me to watch her carefully since he could not put the cast on the way he had planned to. He said she could easily knock the elbow out of socket again and then would require a second surgery. Then he proceeded to tell me that a three-year-old patient of his had to have a second surgery after falling off his tricycle. I really did not need to have that information. Anyhow, we came home the next day. Tara and Lisa had twin beds in their bedroom. I told Lisa she had to rest that afternoon. I later went in to check on her and she was jumping from bed to bed. What's a mother to do!!!!!!!!!!!! She managed to heal and was forbidden to go the neighbor's house to swing. I managed to survive as well with God's help!!!!!! "It is not easy being green," as Kermit the Frog says!!!!!!

Shortly after recovering from her broken elbow, four-year-old Lisa was playing in our fenced-in backyard while I fed Greg. I went out to check on her and the gate was open and there was no Lisa. She had never ventured off before so panic hit me. I walked down the block as I called out her name. She was nowhere in sight. My panic increased as I called out to God to help me find her safe. As I came to the corner, I kept calling out her name. Just then a door opened and Lisa came out from this elderly lady's upstairs apartment. The lady had invited her in for cookies, and even though I had told her never to go into another neighbor's house unless she asked me first, she did just that. I scolded her and escorted her back home. I had been so terrified. God had heard my prayers again.

Just a few months earlier Tara almost drowned. We were visiting Bob's cousin P.J. on a Sunday afternoon when we were invited to go swimming in his pool. I was very pregnant with Greg so there was no way I was going to put on a bathing suit and get into the pool. Bob did not want to either, so the three kids and P.J.'s son jumped into the pool as we sat poolside watching them have fun. All of a sudden I saw seven-year-old Tara go under water. I screamed and Bob jumped in fully clothed to rescue her. She had slipped into the deep end and gone under. She could swim but panicked. She was terrified and did not want to get back into the pool. Bob had to borrow dry clothes and air out his wallet and car keys. Tara told us on the way home that she said an Act of Contrition when she was under water. The Nuns had taught her that if she were ever in danger of dying, she should say the Act of Contrition. That experience was terrifying to all of us. We thanked God for protecting her. Till this day Tara does not care for swimming pools!

A few months later I was waiting on the corner of Calhoun and Willow, the only through street between Holy Name of Jesus School and our house on Calhoun, when Tara and Chris were walking home from school. I was there to make sure they crossed the street safely. Tara was in second grade and Chris was a first-grader. Chris was racing to the corner with a friend of his while Tara was walking a few feet behind him. He was looking at his friend and something told me he was not going to stop at the street. I yelled at him to stop but he did not. A car was coming down Willow as the driver saw me waving my hands and screaming. Chris kept coming right into the street. The driver swerved to avoid hitting him, but managed to knock him down anyway. From my vantage point I could not see whether Chris was knocked down or was under the car. The driver stopped as I ran around the front of his car to see where Chris was. I thought my heart was going to jump right out of my chest. Chris was lying on the street and was trying to get up as I got to him. It was winter so he was wearing a heavy lined jacket with a hood. It seems that the right front bumper had barely hit him but knocked him down. I checked him over and there were no obvious signs of injury. I took the driver's information, then took Chris right over to the Pediatrician's office. Dr. Simon could not find any injuries, but told me what to look for in case of a concussion. Chris had a small bruise on his thigh where the car had grazed him. So I sent him to school the next morning with a note to his teacher in case there was a problem. The school nurse called me about an hour later to tell me that Chris had thrown up. I put Lisa and Greg in the car, and rushed to school then on to Dr. Simon's office. I feared a head injury. Dr. Simon checked him thoroughly, did some tests and told me he thought Chris had a virus or was having a reaction to being knocked down by a car. I prayed that Dr. Simon was right. Chris was fine the next day so my prayers were answered once again. I surely was keeping God busier than usual with my prayers those last few months. I just could not bear the thought of anything happening to my precious children. What an awesome God we have!!!!!!!

Chapter 7 - Transfer to Dallas

Bob, Greg, Liz 1965
Chris, Lisa, Tara

Christmas - 1972
Moulin Menagerie

CHAPTER 7
Transfer to Dallas - Lisa's Surgery

§

"For I, Yahweh, your God, I am holding you by the right
hand, I tell you, 'Do not be afraid, I will help you'."

(*The Jerusalem Bible*, Isaiah 41:13-14)

ON AUGUST 1,1964, WE WERE transferred to Dallas when Greg was 22
months old. It was hard to leave New Orleans where I had lived the first
almost 30 years of my life. My mother came to help for the two weeks
before the move. She spent a lot of the time sitting on the sofa where she
cried and said, "I would never move away from my mother." That made it
even harder for me to leave.

We spent 10 days in motels with 4 children. It was a very trying time.
The first motel we were sent to was a small room with two double beds.
Bob and I slept in one and Tara, Chris and Lisa slept in the second one.
The baby bed for Greg would fit only in front of the bathroom door so every
time someone had to go to the bathroom we had to move the baby bed
whether Greg was asleep or not. The second day I told Bob that we could
not stay there since it would be at least a week before our furniture arrived.
He told his boss what the living arrangements were and asked permission
to move us to another motel where we had two adjoining rooms. It made
it a little easier for Greg to get his naps. As it turned out, it was 10 days

before we could move into the rented house. Those 10 days were very trying, but once again, we made it with God's help!

The very first morning we were in the house Lisa woke up with fever. The landlord had not turned the hot water on, so there was no hot water and Bob could not shave. The movers were there bright and early to unpack our boxes. I had to watch little 22 month old Greg very carefully. He turned the stove on while some boxes were on it and almost started a fire. In exasperation I finally told the movers that I would take care of unpacking the boxes so they were free to go. I was too concerned about finding a Pediatrician to take Lisa to. Bob took her to the doctor's office. He looked grubby since he was unshaven and in work clothes. The office would not take his out-of-town check so he had to pay cash. It was only $4.00 for the visit. Remember this was 1964. Lisa was prescribed an antibiotic for bronchitis. Dr. Keith Robins became our very first friend in Dallas and continued to see the children until they outgrew him. We saw him often for several years.

Tara cried every night because she had had to leave the girls she had been in class with at Holy Name of Jesus School since Kindergarten. The boys and girls at Holy Name were in separate classes. She would be entering 4th grade at a new school and there would be boys in her class as well. She ended up crying and grieving for several months. I secretly cried the first few nights in the motel. I knew that Bob would be traveling every week and that I would be on my own with four little children. I said to the Lord, "OK, Lord! It is going to be You and me! I cannot make it without Your help!" Wow! Did I find out how true that is!!!!

Lisa was sick often. Just a few months after we moved to Dallas she had to have bladder surgery. I felt so alone with no family to help, especially with Bob being gone so much. Bob and I had only each other and the four children to take care of. We made it through with God's help once again.

We rented a house in Farmers Branch so we could become familiar with the area before we bought a house. We had wall to wall furniture in the house and in the garage since we had had large rooms and a much bigger house in New Orleans. It was a Sunday afternoon in April of 1965 when Bob took the children for a ride while I slept off a migraine headache. He came home and asked me to come with them to look at a house. We drove up the driveway to the brick house with columns and I immediately fell in love with the house. We would once again have two bathrooms and room for our furniture in a very nice neighborhood. So, we applied for a G.I. Loan. We were renting a small three bedroom, one bath house for $135.00 per month, and our house payment would be $142.00 per month. The house bordered on the Brookhaven Country Club Golf Course – we thought that was another asset. (We learned that it really was not an asset after 13 broken windows.) The boom was lowered when Bob came home on a Friday with a somber look on his face. He told me that we were turned down for the loan for $20,500.00 because we had four children and not enough income. Our income at the time was $550.00 per month. I was so crushed. Bob said he would go down to the Loan Office and talk to the guy in charge on Monday. I was really desolate that weekend! I kept turning it over to the Lord, then taking it back and grieving. Finally Monday came. Bob called me later in the day and said we were approved for the loan. He talked the Loan Officer into approving us since we had an excellent credit rating and no debt. I immediately gave thanks to God! Once again He came through for me! What an awesome God we have!!!!!!! We moved in May 15th. We have been in this house for 50 years now!

We enrolled Tara for fourth grade, Chris for third grade, and Lisa for morning class Kindergarten in Mary Immaculate Catholic School. Tara, Chris and Lisa were to ride the bus to school. The very first day of school, Lisa, Greg and I were standing outside waiting for the bus to bring the children home. We waited and waited. Finally an hour past the time they were to be dropped off, here came the bus with two very upset children. They had gotten on the wrong bus and had to wait for the other children to be delivered at the farthest point from the school before the bus driver could bring them home. To make matters worse, someone in Tara's fourth grade class asked her if she was a foreigner because of her

New Orleans accent. She did not know what a foreigner was and thought it was not a good thing to be. Bob was out of town for the week and I was alone with three very unhappy children, especially one who did not want to go to school the next day. Fortunately, outgoing Tara soon began to make friends, which eased her pain! The children missed their Daddy every week. So did I!!!!!!!!

There were many visits to the Pediatrician's office over the first ten and a half years of Lisa's life. She was frequently battling upper respiratory infections, but when she felt well, she was playing football with Chris and the neighborhood kids, riding her bike, and was very active. I kept saying that I knew there was something wrong and that someday someone would find it.

When Lisa was ten and a half, she had the flu. I sent her back to school when she recovered, only to have her come home with fever again. We went back to the Pediatrician, who said she had had a relapse and to keep her home for a few more days. I then sent her back to school and the same thing happened again. Back to the doctor we went. He decided to do an ex-ray to check out possible pneumonia. I felt the blood drop down to my feet when Dr. Robins came in, held the x-ray up to the window and said, "My God, there is a big mass of something in this child's chest and it is pushing her heart over to the right. I cannot see a lung on the left. I will have to take this x-ray to the hospital to have a Radiologist read it and will call you." It was 4:00 p.m. in the afternoon. I did not sleep that night.

The next day after I took the kids to school I waited for the doctor to call. I ended up cleaning out my fridge to keep busy. I even cleaned the rims and jar lids. Every time the phone rang I was right there to answer it. I was a nervous wreck all day as I kept praying and cleaning. I picked the children up at school and was afraid I would miss the doctor's call. Rushed home and again waited and prayed. Finally the phone rang at 5:00 p.m. and Dr. Robins told me to take Lisa to the hospital right away to do some tests. I sent the kids to my neighbor's house and called Bob at the office to tell him to meet us at St. Paul's Hospital. I prayed all the way to the hospital.

Lisa was given an upper and lower GI. The doctor came out to tell us that her stomach and intestines were up in the left chest and that her left lung had never expanded. She had no diaphragm on the left side and would need surgery. The diagnosis was a Congenital Diaphragmatic Hernia. While we were very upset with the news, we were grateful to God that finally somebody had found what was wrong and that it was fixable. They confirmed my sense that something was really wrong with Lisa since she was born.

We were sent to a thoracic surgeon Dr. William Taylor. He was appalled that the docs had not found the problem. He let me listen to her chest with his stethoscope. I heard gurgling on the left and breath sounds on the right. If I, a layperson, could distinguish the difference, why could not six Pediatricians do so? So, surgery was scheduled for June. Lisa's side was completely opened up while Dr. Taylor pushed her stomach and intestines back into place and constructed a diaphragm out of muscle and tissue. She was in ICU for three days. I slept on a couch in one of the restrooms so I could go in to see her every four hours. We were finally given a room. Lisa did amazingly well and, by the 9th day, was rolling the wheelchair up and down the hall. Her left lung, which she had never utilized, expanded miraculously. We came home on the 10th day. Our God is a loving and faithful God!

Ten months after surgery Lisa was the first student at Mary Immaculate School to receive the President's Award for Physical Fitness. She is truly a miracle! Most babies born with Congenital Diaphragmatic Hernias usually die at birth. For the past several years surgeons have been doing in-utero surgery to save these babies. I might add that when Lisa had bladder surgery when she was 7 years old, no one picked up on the deformity on the x-ray. I wrote the New Orleans Pediatrician to ask for the x-ray Lisa had had right before we moved to Dallas. He replied saying that the x-ray taken at a prominent hospital had shown the Hernia and that he could not explain how he or the radiologist missed it. I, as a layperson, could see the difference in the right expanded lung compared to the left side, which looked like masses of body tissue. We could have sued and won, but were so grateful that we finally had some answers and that something could be done about it, we decided to let it go. We are so grateful that Lisa made it through those very tough years. Again, isn't our God an Awesome God!!!!!!!!!

Bob continued to travel every week for about three years. It seemed that everything would go wrong or break while he was gone. One cold morning as I got everybody into the car to take the kids to school, Bob's car would not start. It was in the driveway and my car was in the garage. The kids and I pushed his car down the driveway into the street so that I could get my car out of the garage to drive them to school. What I have always believed is that we do what we have to do and God supplies the grace and strength to do so!!!!!!!! A lesson I learned at a very early age!

Chapter 8 - From Kindergarten to College Student

Dear Mrs. Mullins,

For all the things
you've taught us
to learn and do.

Just want you
to know that we
all love you.

A pretty red rose
to brighten your day.
And may God bless
and keep them ever
that way.

"Happy Valentine's Day"

How very nice

How thoughtful, too

Many, many thanks

To you!

"Your Ninty-Six"
Kindergartners
1969-1970

B.S. Degree May, 1977

From Kindergarten Teacher to College Student

§

"Then the Lord answered and said, 'Write the vision down,
inscribe it on tablets to be easily read, since this vision is for
its own time only; eager for its own fulfilment, it does not
deceive; if it comes slowly, wait, for come it will, without fail'. "

(*JERUSALEM BIBLE*, HABAKKUK 2:2-3)

WHEN GREG WAS THREE YEARS old, I enrolled him in an Arts & Crafts class, which my neighbor and friend Lois Small taught. Lois and I became great friends. We saved our newspapers and once a month we would sell them and go for lunch and antiquing. Lois introduced me to antiques, which became one of my hobbies. When she moved away, I took over her little Arts & Crafts Class for three to five-year-olds – a job I thoroughly enjoyed.

When Greg entered First Grade, our Pastor Fr. Robert Vreteau asked me to teach Kindergarten with the Kindergarten teacher Uva Morris. I told him I did not have a college degree other than a Business College Certificate, but was told that Texas did not require a teaching degree for Kindergarten at the time. I accepted the job of teaching art and music in Kindergarten, along with writing, reading and basic math. We had 48 children in the morning class and 48 in the afternoon class. It was a lot of work but so enjoyable. I talked Father Robert into putting a piano in our classroom so I could teach our Kindergartners songs. They learned about 75 songs each year. I was responsible for the art projects and had so much fun coming up with art ideas. Teaching the little Arts & Crafts Class for three years prepared me well. I would finish my job in Kindergartern at 2:00 p.m. and then take the three classes of First Graders for music class on Mondays, the three classes of Second Graders on Tuesdays, and the three classes of Third Graders on Wednesdays. I had found my niche. I firmly believe that music helps students in both reading and math.

I was so in love with teaching after one month in Kindergarten, that I talked to Bob about getting my teaching degree. The following summer I enrolled in Texas Woman's University as a 36 year-old college freshman. I was told by the Advisor assigned to me that I should not be teaching Kindergarten and needed to get my degree as a full-time student. He would not help me with classes, so I picked my own classes. I ended up taking a freshman Biology class, which was used to weed out the weak Nursing Students and an English class, which was used to weed out the weak incoming freshman students. I had studied really hard for the first test in Biology. When the graded test was returned to us after one week of class, I had gotten 29 right out of 60. The negative talk took over and I told myself that I did not belong in college because I was not smart enough and that I belonged home with my pots and pans. I had tears streaming down my cheeks. The little 18 year-old sitting next to me asked what was wrong. I told her that I had been in college for a week and had just flunked out. She asked me my grade and I told her about getting 29 correct out of 60. She said that was good. I said, "Not where I come from!" She said she had gotten the highest grade out of the 124 students and her score was 39 correct out of 60. I said, "You mean I am just 10 points behind you?" To which she nodded her head. I told her, "I think I will stay!" I drove home from Denton with a renewed confidence that I could make it. "Oh! You of little faith!!!!!!!!!!"

I continued to take two classes every summer and do well. Richland Junior College opened up so I decided to get my basics there. After the fourth summer Bob and I made a Marriage Encounter week-end. One of the exercises was to look at our heart's desire. My desire was to go to school full time to get my degree. We had two kids in braces, two in private grade school and Chris at Jesuit College Prep. Tara was at Turner High School. Financially it seemed that we could not make it without my BIG salary of $225.00 per month September through May. Bob and I talked about it and decided that we would try it. I don't know how we did it, but I do know that God multiplied the loaves and the fishes. I gave up having my hair done every week and cut corners in other places. Older women were just beginning to go to college. I was in my upper thirties. I loved school. Still do! I decided to major in Special Education/Elementary Education with endorsements in Kindergarten, Early Childhood Education and Language/Learning Disabilities. I managed to go to school, clean house and cook, drive carpools, and go to the kids' ballgames and activities. My family was a wonderful help and supported me all the way. And my God supplied what we needed!

The fall semester before graduation I was studying for finals when I received a certified letter telling me that I was being sued by some builders. It seems that I had signed a petition going around my neighborhood where we did not want apartments built on the wooded area at the end of our street. Ten people were chosen out of over one hundred on the petition and I was one of the three women on the list – all three of us had the name of Elizabeth. The lawsuit stated that we had had secret meetings with the City Council to block the building of the apartments. I answered the lawsuit telling them that I had a right to sign a petition and that, as far as secret meetings went, I certainly had no time for such meetings since I was teaching full time, going to school in Denton and taking care of a husband, four children, a dog and a house. I was livid when I learned that I had to do more than just write a letter.

I went down to the court so that I could speak to the judge but was told I could not do so. However, his clerk talked to me and told me I had to answer the lawsuit legally, which meant hiring an attorney. I told him that I refused to spend one dime on an attorney and that if he told me what I needed to do, I would do it. He told me I had to write a brief defending my position and file it in court. I asked him where I could get help writing a brief. He kept telling me that I needed an attorney. I insisted that I was going to represent myself. He told me that law students spend a whole semester learning to write briefs. I told him I had 3 weeks in between my semesters and that I was a quick learner. I held my ground so he told me I could go to a law library to look up cases to support my position. The next morning early I was at the SMU law library where I told the young man behind the desk that I needed to write a brief. I asked him to point me in the right direction. I told him why I had to write the brief and he replied that I really needed an attorney and that law students spend a whole semester learning to write briefs. I told him I had three weeks before the spring semester began and I was determined to get that brief written and filed with the court. He shook his head and directed me to the right area. I got a book on writing briefs and followed the procedure.

As I sat in the library day after day that week, law students came up to ask me if I was that lady who was writing a brief and representing herself in a lawsuit. Each one in turn suggested that I get an attorney. I reiterated that I refused to spend money on an attorney. (The other nine people on the lawsuit had hired an attorney to the tune of $1,000 each. I told them I would represent myself. The man who called to tell me about it said I was foolish! I told him that perhaps I was foolish but I was also stubborn!) So I had found quite a few cases to support my stand and was fine tuning my brief when I showed up at the law library the second week in a row. By now everybody there knew me. The young man behind the desk told me that someone wanted to meet me. He pointed to a very well-dressed gentleman sitting nearby. I walked over to him and introduced myself. He told me he was a retired attorney and was fascinated by my case. We visited while I shared my story and then he said, "Mrs. Moulin, I want to represent you. I cannot do it free, though, but if you can afford $5.00, I will take over!" He also shared that he had been one of the Army lawyers who was involved with the Nuremberg trials after World War II. He asked me to give him what I had researched and written so far. He looked at it and, to my surprise, he said it was pretty good. Then he said, "Let's go do more research and I will show you how to fine tune what you have written." I spent the next few days meeting him at the library and working with him. He was a delightful man in his 70's. We finished the brief and he took it from there. He went to the hearing to represent me and then called to tell me that the lawsuit was dropped. In spite of all the aggravation I endured by being sued, I learned a lot and met a delightful person who helped me when I needed it. This is just another example of how God has taken care of me all of my life. He always provides the help I need!

I was 43 years old when I graduated in May, 1977, and was hired by the Carrollton/Farmers Branch School District, where I taught Early Childhood Handicapped, as it was labeled at the time. My class consisted of three, four and five-year-old students, who were learning disabled, physically handicapped, emotionally disturbed, and borderline mentally retarded. I loved my students. The last year I taught special education, my fifth year, I had a self-contained class of First through Fifth graders with the same issues as the younger children. It was challenging. By this time I had gotten my Master's Degree as an Educational Diagnostician and Special Ed Supervisor and Elementary Ed Supervisor. My Master's Paper was a "Handbook for Parents of Early Childhood Handicapped." I published it and sold over 500 copies. The TWU Bookstore sold it as well.

That Master's Paper was truly a gift from God. I had done all my research, had books from three libraries strewn on my dining room table, and was ready to start writing when Bob came home on a Thursday with a very somber look on his face. I was making Swedish meatballs for dinner when I asked what was wrong. After hesitating, he told me that he had been to the doctor and was told that he might have a brain tumor or perhaps had had a stroke according to some tests. I have to interject here that Bob had lost his job the previous March when his company was bought out by another. He had been an Assistant Vice President and now he was unemployed. His news threw me into anger and fear. I was ready to give up my

Master's! I was angry with God, angry with Bob, angry with myself, angry with life!!!! I told Bob, "God has gone too far this time! I cannot bear the thought of your being ill and maybe dying and leaving me behind! I cannot do this! I am going to drop out of school." Bob held me and told me that I had to finish this Master's, which would mean $1,000.00 a year more in pay. Besides I had done all the research and now all I had to do was write.

I cried myself to sleep that night as I poured out my anger and fear to God. I told Him that I could not cope with this latest crisis. I put my feelings aside and went to my classroom the next day. When I came home from school on Friday, Bob asked for my grocery list and told me that he and kids would take care of the house, the meals, and the laundry so that I would be free to write the whole week-end. I told him I was giving up and would not be writing! He kept encouraging me, but in my stubbornness I sat in front of the TV all evening trying to block out my feelings. On Saturday morning I got up, sat at the dining room table and sobbed as I looked at all of the research. Then I gave in as I usually do after a battle with God and said, "Lord, if You want this done, then You will have to do it! I have nothing in me right now!" I dried my tears, blew my nose, and put the pen to paper. The "Handbook" was born after many labor pains! I spent the next two week-ends writing while Bob and the children pitched in. At last, it was finished. On that Monday Bob repeated the tests he had had earlier and miraculously there was no evidence that he had had a tumor or a stroke. Whether the original tests were wrong or Bob had had a miracle, we know that God was working in this situation. Once more in my life my God had come through for me! How can I ever doubt or be afraid!!!!!!!

After being unemployed for 368 days, Bob was hired by a bank where he made about one-third his original salary at Associates. We were so grateful to God that he had a job. We knew it would be a stretch for our budget, but we also knew that somehow we would make it with God's help. Little did we know how trying that job would be. Bob's patience was challenged in this new job as he worked for a tyrant of a boss. He endured nine years of put-downs and abuse until we prayed the situation away. His boss finally got transferred to another department. Prayers were answered.

Chapter 9 - Special Ed Teacher

My Special Kids 1979

Classroom 1977

CHAPTER 9

Special Education Teacher

§

"Trust in Yahweh and do what is good, make your home
in the land and live in peace; make Yahweh your only
joy and he will give you what your heart desires.

(*THE JERUSALEM BIBLE*, PSALM 37:3-4)

MY FIRST YEAR IN SPECIAL Ed was in Early Childhood Handicapped as it was called at the time. I had 8 precious little three, four and five- year -old children with Language/Learning Disabilities, Physical Handicaps, Autism, and Developmentally Delayed. My class consisted of 7 little boys and 1 little girl. I had a part-time Aide who was wonderful to work with. I did ask to have Carolyn full-time because I had to change the three-year-old's diapers. I encountered quite a dilemma because I could not leave my 7 boys and take her to the girls' bathroom, which we shared with the 5th and 6th graders on the wing and the other four Special Ed Classes. I could not change her diaper in front of the little boys and I would not send her home with a soiled diaper. When I met with my Supervisor and asked for more Aide time, she said to me, "Can't you potty-train that child?" I very calmly said, "Spina Bifida children cannot be potty-trained!" I was then on the Supervisor's black list. I suppose I unintentionally embarrassed her since, as a Special Ed Supervisor, she should have known that info. So, I did not start off well with her. She refused to give me more Aide time. Bob and I found a very large appliance box, cut it up, painted it and taped it together to form a screen, which was perfect for changing the diapers. I positioned the screen so that the child could not be seen but that I could see the other students. My little autistic student was prone to running out of the classroom, so I had to be on my guard constantly. I am grateful that God gave me the grace to find a way to solve problems.

I encountered resistance from the Principal that year as well. He was not too fond of our special kids as I learned when I overheard him say that he would rather not have us in his school. I know what it is like to "fight city hall." I firmly believed that music would be very helpful to our Special Ed Students, so I asked if the five classes could be included in the music program. I was given a firm "NO." So, I found out when the music room was vacant and arranged with the other Special Ed teachers to take the five classes for music since I could play the piano. We then put on a music program for the parents, the Special Ed Director and anyone who wanted to come. It was a great success and our Special Kids loved it. So did the parents! I do believe that the challenges I experienced growing up prepared me to accept the challenges I encountered in later years!

My second year of teaching Special Ed I was sent to another school to be housed there until a new school was finished in a couple of months. I was introducing myself to the teachers there when a 6th grade teacher said that she would not bother getting to know me since I would be there for a short time. My reply to her was, "That's too bad because I am nice to know!" I ended up staying at that school the whole year thanks to Marie Huie, the Principal and the former Special Ed Director, who had hired me. That teacher never did bother to get to know me.

I am so grateful to know that the Holy Spirit lives within me and guides me daily. This was so evident one morning as I asked my Aide to check with the office about a little student who had not shown up for class. His mother had always called to report his absence. My Aide learned that his mother had not called that morning so she called the mother. The mother told her that she had put R on the bus that morning and became alarmed when told that R was not in my class. My Aide then called the bus depot and asked them to check the bus. Sure enough, R had fallen asleep on the bus and the driver had not seen him at the back of the bus. Fortunately he had been in the parked school bus for a little over an hour on a very cool day. I seemed to know that something was wrong and thanked God for putting it on my heart to check on R's absence. Thank God it was not a hot Texas day! I was made even more aware of how important it is to listen to that still small voice within!

I went to Marie when I was told by the Librarian that I would not be allowed to bring my kids to the library to look at books because they were Special Ed. She said they would wreck her library, tear up books, and create havoc. I told her they would be better behaved than the regular ed children. She still refused, so I took the problem to Marie. That afternoon my class was in the library being taught by me how to pick out a book, sit at the table and look at their books. We were very systemic in our approach. The Librarian was amazed at how well behaved my little special kids were.

Marie Huie came to my rescue again when I was told that I would be moving to a temporary building on the new school grounds while the school was being completed. I would have had to get my 8 little ones out of the temporary classroom, go down steps to get to the bathrooms in another temporary building. My little Spina Bifida student had fallen and was in a body cast, which meant I had to carry her. It was difficult enough to pick her up and carry her outside when we had fire drills. I really did not know how I would be able to put coats on everyone, keep them in tow, walk down the steps and up again and carry Amy. I was still without a full-time Aide. So again I went to Marie and asked her to ask my new Principal to let me stay where I was until the school was ready. He was not happy about my request but let me stay. I had another little autistic student who would dash out the door in a flash, in addition to another little one whose mother had been on drugs all during pregnancy. She had a lot of hallucinations. Half of my class had been with me the year before. The other half were new to the program.

The new school was completed in April. My new Principal came to my classroom to tell me to pack up and move. I had spent months getting my little students comfortable with our routine. They were doing so well. I knew that a move this late in the year would undo all the progress we had made, especially my little autistic students for whom change threw them into a tizzy. I voiced my concern to my new Principal and was told to "just deal with it!" Once again I went to Marie Huie and pleaded my case. And once again Marie came to my rescue. I was granted permission to finish out the two months left in the school year, then move to the new school. My new Principal was upset with me. I did not win favor with him. What was best for my little ones came first! I was willing to pick up my slingshot if I had to slay the giant!!!!!!! I spent the next two years at this new school.

I learned so much from my special little children. One of them stands out in my memory. He came into my classroom early that first day of school. He walked over to my desk, kicked it and said, "I hate you, desk!" Then he walked around the room as he knocked the books and toys over and re-peated the same words. As he walked up to me to kick me, too, I told him that I thought he needed a hug. I bent down and hugged a very stiff little four-year-old who reeked of urine. G was a bed wetter and had apparently slept in his clothes. He also threw up just bile shortly after I hugged him. I knew then that he had not had breakfast. So I took him to the cafeteria to get something to eat. We had this routine every morning from then on. I would have something for him to eat, then I would put him on my lap and hold him until the other children arrived. As I held him I prayed for the grace to tolerate that my clothes would smell like urine the rest of the day because what this child needed more than anything was to know that he was loved. That is what I was called to do. I set up a parent/teacher conference with his mother, who had been married several times and was around 30 years old. She stood me up at 7:00 in the morning. I learned that his older sister was in the Emotionally Disturbed class at another school.

Some of G's behaviors continued for a few weeks. I would put him in time-out, then hug him afterwards as I reiterated that hitting, kicking, punching other children or destroying things would not be acceptable in my classroom. It was around Halloween when he came over to me, put his arms around my legs, looked up at me and said, "Teacher, I love you!" Wow! I had to fight back tears! Those hugs made a difference. It is unfortunate that in today's world teachers are not allowed to show affection for fear of being accused of sexual abuse.

The story goes on. Three years later, after I had resigned my teaching job, I received a phone call from a second grade teacher who told me that she had G in her class. She told me that he had been acting out one day, so she told him that she thought that what he needed was a hug. She said she hugged him and he said, "My teacher, Mrs. Moulin, used to hug me every day!" She just wanted me to know that he remembered those hugs! Marie Huie had suggested that she call me. My heart was dancing with joy as I thanked God for giving me the grace to tolerate the awful smell of urine and to love this little boy. There is more! Two years after this incident I received a phone call from a teacher in another school district. She told me that G had come to school with a bruised throat with hand prints on him. She said she had heard that I taught him in Early Childhood and that he had mentioned my name. She called CPS to report the incident, so they went over to the apartment the next day to talk to the parents, but the family had moved out with no forwarding address. That was the last I heard of G. I am grateful to those teachers who called me. I did not know either of them but they tracked me down. God is good! In the thirty years since I sometimes think of G and ask God to protect him wherever he is. This child really touched my heart deeply!

I originally thought I would teach Kindergarten forever until I began teaching Special Education. Then I thought I would teach Special Ed forever until I had breast cancer my fourth year teaching Special Ed. Now that I had my Master's Degree, I began to re-evaluate my life. I began the discernment prayer. Where to now, God? I somehow knew it was time to leave the classroom. I loved testing children. I had a gift for it, so I applied for a Diagnostician's job three times my fifth year in the District. And three times someone less qualified than I got the jobs. I had a successful Special Ed Class and the powers that be would not let me out of it. Needless to say, I was crushed because I knew it was time to move on, but where I did not know!

After much prayer and discernment it was very clear that my classroom days were over. I did not want to apply in another School District so I drove up to TWU to check out what jobs might be available. As I was talking to the College of Education Secretary, I said out of the blue, "I wonder what it would take for me to get certified as a Counselor!" That thought had never come into my mind before, so I knew it must be the Holy Spirit talking. Nancy told me to send my transcript to Dr. Sparks, who was the Dean of the College, and she would let me know. I very gingerly mentioned to Bob that I was considering returning to TWU for possibly another Master's Degree. I say gingerly because he and the kids were really concerned about my health and my incurring any stress in life since I had had cancer. I assured them that I loved school and the only stress would be in trying to get everything done at home. They once again agreed to help.

Dr. Sparks sent me a letter with the requirements of 20 hours of courses since many of the hours from my first Master's would count toward certification in Counseling & Guidance. I said, "Oh! I can do that!" So, I once again enrolled in TWU. I tutored to earn money and again juggled all the balls in the air with God's help and my family's help. I am convinced that when we seek God's Will and then do His Will, everything seems to fall into place.

I was almost through the 20 hours when Texas decided that if one wanted to be in private practice as a therapist, one would need a Master's in Counseling and Guidance. Then take a State Board Exam in order to be licensed after completing 2,000 hours of supervised counseling. Since I had decided that this was the route I planned to take, I asked what I would have to do to get a Master's in the field. Dr. Sparks told me that I would have to write a thesis. I said, "Oh! I can do that!" ("I can do all things through Him who strengthens me!") So, I collected materials from four libraries on breast cancer, treatment, reconstructive surgery, and self-image and began my thesis. Half way through the thesis I learned that I did not have to have another Master's Degree but that my 20 hours of classwork and my taking the State Board Exam after completing my 2,000 hours would suffice. Well, I decided that since I had worked hard on putting the thesis together, I might as well finish it. Thus, the second Master's was earned. While I have many letters behind my name, it is very humbling to know that the first letters I received were B.S.!!!!!!

Chapter 10 - Breast Cancer

2/1/1981

CHAPTER 10
Breast Cancer & Cancer Work

"We are only the earthenware jars that hold this treasure, to
make it clear that such an overwhelming power comes from
God and not from us. We are in difficulties on all sides;
but never cornered; we see no answer to our problems, but
never despair; we have been persecuted; but never deserted;
knocked down, but never killed; always, wherever we may
be, we carry with us in our body the death of Jesus, so that
the life of Jesus, too, may always be seen in our body.

Indeed, while we are still alive, we are consigned to
our death every day, for the sake of Jesus, so that in
our mortal flesh the life of Jesus, too, may be openly
shown. So death is at work in us, but life in you."

(THE JERUSALEM BIBLE, 2 CORINTHIANS 4:7-12)

I REALLY ENJOYED FRIDAYS. BOB and I had our date night on Fridays. We
went out for dinner and a movie. As I lay in bed this particular January
night in 1981, I thought of all the things I needed to do that week-end. I
was feeling really good about my life. I loved my teaching job. My children
were practically grown. Greg was a senior at Jesuit. Tara had finished college and was married and living in California. Chris and Lisa were working. We were in the home stretch with raising our family. Greg would be

going off to Texas A & M in the fall and we would then be empty-nesters. I was at peace! Then I remembered that it was time to check my breasts. As I moved my hand around the right breast I felt a small lump high up as the breast began. I checked the left breast but could not find a matching lump. I don't know why I was thinking that it would be OK if I had a matching lump on the left side. My peace flew out the window as fear settled over me like a dark cloud engulfing me. I couldn't sleep because I kept checking the lump and somehow wishing that it would disappear.

The week-end before, *The Dallas Morning News* had published a whole section on breast cancer and reconstruction surgery. I remember telling Bob as I read the paper that I hoped I would never have to deal with breast cancer because I did not think I could handle it. He told me that I certainly could handle it just as I have handled everything else in my life. I told him I would be a basket case if that happened to me. So, here it was just a few days later and I am discovering a lump in my breast. Because it was a Friday night I would have to wait until Monday morning to call my doctor. I did get a lot of things done that week-end just so I could keep busy while I tried not to think. Besides praying unceasingly, keeping busy was my way of coping with fear and stress. I kept pleading with the Lord to let this lump be nothing to worry about.

Monday morning I called my OB/GYN's office to see when I could come in to have him check my breast. The receptionist told me that he was booked solid for two weeks. I told her that I had found a lump in my breast and was anxious to have it checked out and could she please fit me in as soon as possible. She asked me to hold on while she checked with the doctor, then came back to tell me that he could not see me for two weeks. I was crushed. I could not wait two weeks to find out what it was. So I called my beloved Internist Dr. Jerry Kaumo, who told me to come in that afternoon. I was glad to be teaching that day since it distracted me from totally focusing on the lump. I am grateful that God has always given me the grace to do the tasks at hand.

I left school immediately after class ended. The nurse took me in right away. At first Jerry could not find anything since he had told me not to tell him which side and where the lump was. After several tries he said he could not find anything. I told him to go higher where the breast began. He did and there it was! He sent me right over for a Mammogram. The Radiologist came out to tell me he found nothing so I would have to go back in for another one. He then checked for the lump and found it after I told him to go higher. He did and it showed up on the x-rays. I am sharing this because if I had not checked high enough, I would not have found the lump myself and checked it out. You really don't want to miss a lump!

Jerry Kaumo was calling as I walked in the door. The Radiologist had told him that the lump looked suspicious so I would need a surgeon. Jerry asked me what kind of surgeon I wanted and I told him I wanted someone who was an excellent surgeon with a good bedside manner. A few days later I was in the surgeon's office as he reviewed my options. Surgeons had just begun to do lumpectomies but there were no studies comparing the survival rates between women who had had mastectomies and those who had had lumpectomies. He recommended that I have a mastectomy if it turned out to be cancer. In those days biopsies were usually not done until the patient went into surgery in case a mastectomy would be required immediately. So I did not know what to expect.

I had a week to prepare for the hospital stay. I somehow knew I had cancer but kept dismissing that idea. I prayed unceasingly for the courage to face whatever I had to face. I was admitted to the hospital on Sunday afternoon for surgery on Monday. A group of friends from my church came to pray with me. One of the men asked me what Psalm I would like him to read. I thought of the 23rd Psalm, but immediately thought I don't want to go to the valley of death, so out of the blue I told him to read Psalm 138. I really did not know what that Psalm was. It just popped out of my mouth. God works in mysterious ways!!!!! Psalm 138 is very short. The last paragraph of it says, "Though I live surrounded by trouble, You will preserve my life!" (*Jerusalem Bible*) Wow! Did I take those words to heart! Whenever I woke up during the night, I prayed those words. I prayed them all the way into surgery until I was put to sleep. When I finally woke up from the anesthesia, I asked Bob if it was cancer. He said it was. Then I felt my chest. My right breast was gone. I was then too nauseated to really feel the impact of that moment! I remember Greg holding the pan while I threw up. Bob gently wiped my brow. Lisa stood by looking terrified and helpless!

Once I woke up I was amazed that I was not as devastated as I thought I would be. As visitors came into the room, they, too, were amazed to find that my spirits were up. There was no somber attitude here. My doctor commended me for having such a good attitude. That attitude did not come from me but from the grace that God poured out on me. My friend Sr. Joan called that morning to ask how I was doing. I told her it was cancer. She said that while I was in surgery the Sisters were praying for me and their prayer was Psalm 138! Isn't God amazing!!!!!! I came home the following Saturday. I had not taken any pain pills at all while I was in the hospital. Besides the modified radical mastectomy, twenty lymph nodes were removed from under my arm. I was doing great! No pain! I even put in a load of wash in the washing machine when I got home – much to my family's dismay!

Then Monday morning's awakening hit me like a ton of bricks! The pain under my arm was excruciating. I could not lift my arm. It was the coldest day of the winter and I was scheduled to have a bone scan plus a surgeon's visit to remove the two drains coming from my chest. Lisa drove me to St. Paul's Hospital for the bone scan at 8:00 a.m. She had to help me dress that morning. She was terrified that something was really wrong since I had not been in pain. Lying on the hard table for the bone scan was so painful. I prayed my way through it. I just wanted to go home, crawl into bed, and pull the covers over my head. I, too, was thinking that something must be very wrong. My surgeon's appointment was at 10:00 a.m. When we arrived at his office, we were told that he had an emergency surgery and I would have to come back to the office at 1:00 p.m. I was almost in tears. The pain was worse by this time. There was not enough time to go home and come back, so we decided that I could lie on the couch in the waiting room since no one else was in there. Lisa offered to get me something to eat but I was afraid I would throw up. It was a long three-hour wait! Finally my name was called about 1:15 p.m. I wanted to burst into tears when the doctor walked in but I held back. I told him about the pain and he assured me that this was normal. He said the nerves had been asleep and were now awake. He asked if I had filled the prescription for pain pills. I told him I had not because I had not had any pain until that day. He removed the drains and sent me home with the good news that there was no lymph node involvement. I was to see a Radiologist that week to set up my radiation schedule. Lisa wanted to drive me right home then pick up the pain meds. I asked her to stop on the way to get my pills. I don't like taking meds, especially pain pills, but was eager to get one down so that I could get some relief! As the days went on, the pain lessened.

I was told to start the exercises the doctor had given me so that I would regain the complete use of my right arm. I had tears in my eyes as I did the painful exercises but they paid off in a few weeks. I did regain full use of my arm. (About a year later I developed lymphedema in that arm and was fitted with a custom-made compression sleeve. The swelling went down in a few months. I was relieved that I would not have to deal with this problem indefinitely.)

The following Monday – just two weeks since surgery – my good friend Cathy Oldham drove me to St. Paul's Hospital to get evaluated for the radiation I would start. I met with the Radiologist and Nurse Tech to be marked with a red marker just where I would be radiated. A black "x" was placed where my cancerous tumor was. As I lay on the table after the marking of my body, the doctor grabbed a camera and proceeded to take a picture of my chest. My immediate reaction was to pull the sheet over my chest and yell at him. I stopped myself and let my sense of humor come through. I said, "I'll bet the playgirl of the month does not feel like this when she is getting photographed." No one laughed! I was there about two and one-half hours and neither the doctor nor the tech laughed at any jokes I made. I felt like a lump of meat on a butcher block. The doctor had no bed-side manner at all. They both talked over me and not to me.

I was terrified about being there and would have appreciated some TLC but got none!

After the doctor left the room I told the nurse tech how frightened I was and wondered why both she and the doctor were so impersonal. She replied, "Well, honey, we lose a lot of patients so we cannot let ourselves get emotionally involved with them." I said, "Well, honey, you are not going to lose this patient!"

I showed up the next Monday not knowing what to expect. I was escorted into a room where the large machine awaited me. The Tech strapped me onto the very hard table and directed the radiation machine directly over the marked areas across my shoulder blade, the right breast, and down my sternum. She told me to be perfectly still. I was afraid to even breathe. Then she closed the very thick door as I began to hear a loud buzzing sound. Tears started to flow as though I had just turned on a faucet. I was absolutely terrified! All I could do was say, "Lord, help me get through this nightmare, please! I am so scared!" I don't remember how long the radiation treatment lasted, but it seemed like a very long time in spite of being a short time! As I was getting off the table after the Tech released me from the straps, I noticed mummy-like casts in one corner in various sizes. Some seemed small enough for babies. Others were larger! I asked the tech what the casts were for. She told me that they use them to put over babies and children to strap them on the table because there was no way they could be still otherwise. I could only imagine how terrifying that would be to little ones to be restrained in that way. I wondered how little ones could endure radiation therapy if I, an adult, was so terrified! I cried all the way home that day! I asked the Lord to give those little ones comfort!

At the time there was both a smoking and a non-smoking waiting room at St. Paul's. Very often I was the only patient in the non-smoking waiting room. The smoking waiting room was filled with patients who were diagnosed with different cancers as they waited for their radiation treatments. I was baffled that someone who had cancer, especially lung cancer, would be doing radiation and still puffing away on a cigarette.

My routine for five weeks was to teach my Early Childhood Special Ed students until noon, check in with the sub who came in, then drive to St. Paul's for radiation. I would get home about three o'clock and immediately take a nap. Bob would wake me for dinner about 6 and by 8 o'clock I was back in bed for the night. One of the side effects of radiation therapy is extreme fatigue. As the weeks went on I became more and more tired. I had never experienced such fatigue before in my whole life!

After the first week of radiation I felt an itching on my back. Bob looked at my back and told me that I had a red burn in the shape of an upside "L." It happened to match the radiation marks on my chest. When I asked the Tech about the burn, she told me that the radiation goes right through the body and burns whatever is in its way. About this time I began to have difficulty swallowing food, even water. My esophagus was also being burned. It was like swallowing broken up razor blades every time I swallowed anything. I lived on shakes, puddings, and jello. It was difficult to keep going, but perseverance is one of my strongest characteristics, thanks be to God! My faithful Lord gave me the grace and courage to endure as He always had!

I am glad that radiation therapy has improved since those days. Thirty-four years later I am paying the price for it with a damaged lung, damaged heart, and damaged liver. Did it save my life? I will never know. Since I did not have any lymph node involvement, it is impossible to say whether I really needed radiation or not. What I do know is that I am still very much alive!

There were times when I would be driving down the street and would burst into tears. I did not know what was wrong with me until one day I realized that I was grieving. Breast cancer not only took away a precious part of my body but also took away the security I had felt by being a healthy and active 46 year old. It was as though I would now walk around with a big black cloud over my head. One day as I was praying I visualized myself under this cancer cloud and told the Lord that I refused to live with this ugly cloud following me around. I made the decision to ride that cloud. I visualized myself getting a ladder and climbing on top of it! I had been wondering how long I would live. A couple of people had asked me how long I had. I looked at my watch and said, "Oh! Anywhere from a couple of seconds to hopefully 30 or 40 years or more!" People can be so insensitive! I was also asked what had I done wrong that God punished me in this way!!!!!!!! WOW! I found myself defending God! God did not cause my cancer! Another attitude I discovered was that some people thought that God sent me cancer because He knew I could handle it and because He loved me more than others! Now, that is one for the books!!!!!!!!!!! I suppose these people thought they were comforting me in some strange way!

It amazes me how often we find out who our true friends are. I had a phone call one morning from a friend who chastised me for being down. I had earlier gone into the closet to get dressed and realized that there were some blouses I could not wear unless I pinned them up high or else the breast prosthesis would show. What hit me was that the freedom to put on any of my clothes had been taken away from me. It was just another grief with which to deal. So when my friend called me and asked how I was feeling, I related the incident in the closet and told her that I was sad. She told me that I had exactly 10 seconds to feel sorry for myself, that I needed to get over it. I always bristle when my feeling reality is dismissed so I said to her, "These are my feelings and my grief and I will decide how long I will have them!" I never heard from this "good" friend again. I was shamed for grieving my loss!

I have to admit that I wondered how long I would live. A few months after my diagnosis and surgery I was talking to the Lord about my dreams and goals. I told Him that I wanted to live to see Greg graduate from Jesuit, then Texas A & M. I wanted to see my first grandchild, learn to paint, spend many more years with Bob and my family, etc., etc., etc. What happened then was that I saw myself ten years down the road. What I heard in my heart was, "Liz, if you worry about when you are going to die, you will be wasting your life! Leave it to me and go live your life!" WOW! I made the resolve to make the most of each day I had. One of my mottos is, "Be mindful to the moment, Liz! You will never have this moment again! Surrender your life to the Lord!" With God's grace I have done my best to live that motto.

Two years after my diagnosis I became a Reach to Recovery Volunteer for the American Cancer Society. I visited women who had had mastectomies or lumpectomies before they were discharged from the hospital. The very first patient I visited was so devastated. She was crying profusely and asking me "Why, why did this have to happen to me?" I took her hand and looked into her eyes and said, "Well, if it had not happened to me, I could not be here helping you now."

She was amazed to see that I looked good in my clothes, was active in life, and looked healthy. I walked out of that hospital room with a sense of having completed my grief journey. I certainly would not have wished breast cancer on anyone, but now I could see the blessing in my having had breast cancer. I could now give other women hope that they, too, could recover and lead good, productive lives. God has surely blessed me! I did cancer work for 5 years after which I resigned to build my private therapy practice. I cannot tell you how often a new patient would come in to see me and start off telling me she was dealing with breast cancer while not knowing that I am a survivor. It also happens when I give retreats! I am always in awe at how God recycles garbage into grace! God has been recycling man's garbage into grace since Adam and Eve. You might say that He had the first recycling plant!

I continued to give talks to doctors in training at the Medical School and nursing students at the Nursing Schools. I was thrilled to let them know how they could best serve breast cancer patients. I stressed the importance of bed-side manner and not hiding from their emotions. I also stressed the importance of recognizing that there is a normal grief process that occurs after a diagnosis of breast cancer with the subsequent surgery and treatment. I considered my cancer work a ministry – another way to help heal the Body of Christ!

Chapter 11 - Lightning Strikes Again

Bob 1991

Greg, Lisa, Chris, Tara
Our Children

Lightning Strikes a Second Time

§

"It is the Lord who marches before you; he will be with you and
will never fail you or forsake you. So do not fear or be dismayed."

(*THE NEW AMERICAN BIBLE*, DEUTERONOMY 31:8)

I HAD OPENED MY PRIVATE practice in 1984 and was doing well. I leased an
office in a therapy center for 6 years, then opened my own office, which I
shared with my friend Edgerly Lindsley. Bob was working at the bank. I
had recovered from breast cancer, reconstructive surgery and was feeling
well. I came home one evening from my office and as I walked into the
house, I saw boxes on the table. I looked in them and recognized items
from Bob's desk at the bank. I walked into the computer room where he
sat, took one look at him and knew he was very upset. He had gone into
work that Monday morning and a meeting of his department was called at
3:00 p.m. He and 100 employees were told that the bank was closing their
department, which was the recovery department for delinquent Master
and Visa charge accounts, and they were to pack up their desks and leave.
There had been no warning whatsoever. I thought I was having a nightmare. Bob was 61 years old and it had taken him 368 days to find a job
when he was 49. We were hit hard by this turn of events. He had planned
to work until he was 65 years old. Now we would have a struggle to make
ends meet with just my income. We had been there before 13 years earlier

and I was not ready to deal with tightening the belt at this stage in my life. I was thrown into desolation. I could not believe that this was happening a second time. How could lightning strike us a second time????? I cried myself to sleep as I begged God for the strength to deal with this crisis and to be a support to Bob, who was also devastated. Needless to say I did not sleep very much that night. I had to drive Bob down to the bank the next morning to pick up the items he could not carry on the bus. He took the bus downtown to work every day. He was very silent. I did not know what to say – an unusual experience for me! I just kept asking the Lord to help us come up with a plan.

We waited until the week-end to sit down and discuss how we could work the budget and what Bob could do to generate income. Since he was approaching 62 in a few months, he decided that it would help if he took early Social Security and early retirement. Then we discussed what jobs he might be able to do. He tried several things that first year but none panned out. We had to realize that vacations would be out and that less money would be going into our retirement account. The Bank did not have 401K's at the time, so the retirement check would be meager. We would also have to take on the medical insurance premium, which ended up costing more than the retirement check. With God's help we managed to adjust to our new lifestyle. We had never been extravagant and knew how to do with less. God does multiply the loaves and the fishes for sure! We saw that happen over and over again!!!!!

Bob announced to me one day that he was going to be a Volunteer Chaplain at the hospital, which was RHD and is now Dallas Medical Center. He has been a volunteer for 22 years now. He has helped so many patients and families as they dealt with illness, surgery and death. His gentle and caring spirit is such a comfort to those who are hurting in some way. He has brought Jesus to so many people over the years. One story among many that touches my heart is when Bob, at the hospital one day, decided to start down at the end of the hall and work his way back. Just as he started down the hall, he said something inside him told him to start at the first room instead. So he turned around and went to the very first room. He walked in to see several members of a family standing around the patient's bed. He had visited the patient several times before as he was in and out of the hospital. The man was lucid so Bob asked him if he wanted Communion and he nodded "yes". Bob prayed with the family and gave all of them Communion. Then he started down the hall again. He had gotten three rooms down when one of the sons of the patient came running after him. He said, "Thank you for giving my father Communion. He smiled and took his last breath right after. My dad loved the Eucharist! He died in perfect peace!" Bob said that chills ran down his spine as he thought what if he had not listened to that quiet, small voice deep within and had gone down to the end of the hall first. God works in mysterious ways. Bob felt so blessed to have been able to participate in this man's death. There are many more stories I could share with you. What a blessing my husband has been to me, our family and all those whose lives he has touched over the years and continues to touch. I am a very blessed woman!

Front: Alez, Tara, Joe, Melissa and Adam Arciniega
Rear: Emily, Levi, Landry and Jesse Lashbrook

Matt, Faith, Rebecca, Becca, Michael, Jessica
Danene and Chris Moulin

Liz Moulin, Lisa Kupersmith,
And Bob Moulin

In memory of Paul Kupersmith

Greg, Leticia, Forrest & D Moulin

Blake & Kelsey Martin, Greg & D Moulin

CHAPTER 12

Adult Children, Marriages, Grandchildren & Great-Grandchildren

§

"By this love you have for one another, Everyone
will know that you are my disciples."

(*THE JERUSALEM BIBLE*, JOHN 13:35)

OUR FIRST-BORN TARA KEPT US hopping with school activities. She was our social butterfly from the very beginning. In grade school she played guitar with a group of girls. High school was busy with drill team, drama and cheerleading. Her first year of college was spent at Stephen F. Austin in Nagodoches, Texas, where she majored in Psychology her first semester. She was also interested in Theater, which was her major the second semester. The Drama Department was offering try-outs for the different parts in "The Night Thoreau Spent in Jail," so Tara tried out not for just any part but for the lead. As she sat in the auditorium waiting for her turn, a senior girl asked her what part was she going to audition for and she told her the lead. The girl then said to her that freshmen never get leads in the plays. Lo and behold! Tara got the lead. The practice went on for several weeks before the week-end performance. We were not able to attend the play but the reviews were great. Since she was a baby we had called her Sarah Bernhardt (a famous actress in the 30's) so we knew she could act. She also had a major dance role in another production that year. We were thrilled that she was using the gifts God had given her.

Between practice and studies Tara had no time to do her laundry, so she kept buying new underwear every week. When she finally came home at the end of the semester, the whole backseat of the car was nothing but bags of dirty laundry. She decided that summer to enroll in the Dance Department at North Texas University. She was always interested in so many areas, but finally decided on a degree in Criminal Justice from University of Texas Arlington. Tara did her internship with the Dallas Juvenile Department and continued to volunteer there where she worked with troubled teen girls for six years. I remember her visiting my special ed class and asking me how I could work with my special kids with so many problems. I looked at her and said that I could not work with teenage offenders the way she does. We both laughed. That is why we have so many different flavors of ice cream! We are each uniquely made and given special gifts by God to use to help build the Body of Christ.

In summers and holidays Tara worked at Tupinamba Mexican Restaurant where she met the handsome manager Joe Arciniega. They were married April 29, 1978. Joe won us over from the very beginning, but really cinched the deal when I came home the Monday after the wedding to find a beautiful bouquet of flowers with the note that said, "Dear Mom & Dad, Thank you for the beautiful wedding! I want you to know that your daughter will be well loved and cared for! Love, Your New Son Joe!" He was in for sure!!!!!! After 36 years he has lived up to his promise and more! Joe is another son to us.

A couple of years after they were married Joe had an opportunity to move to Los Angeles to work with his Dad in his tax office. We were happy for them but sad for us. California was a far piece away. Tara got a job working in the counseling office at Robert Schuller's Hour of Power. We saw them at Christmas and in the summer.

Joe called one evening to ask if we could rearrange the furniture in the bedroom where they stayed when they came to visit. I naively asked why. Then he said because when they came at Christmas, we would need to make room for a baby bed. I was so excited that I could hardly contain my joy! Tara and Joe had been married for 6 years so we were anxiously awaiting a grandchild. Emily Rose was born on September 27, 1984. We hopped a plane to LA the day before Tara was to come home with Emily. Tara was surprised because she did not know her Dad was coming, too. Then the day I drove Bob to the airport to return to Dallas, I waited an hour for Lisa's flight to come in. She had to see her first-born little niece. Both Tara & Joe were surprised again when Lisa appeared at their patio door. She stayed for a few days. What a joy to hold my first grandchild. I was happy to spend two weeks with them. I soaked up my new role as a grandmother! I lamented the distance between Texas and California, though! Christmas seemed a long time to wait to spoil my precious Emily.

Emily and I have many wonderful memories of spending time together once they moved to Tyler, Texas. I would sit her on the counter as I made cakes, cookies, or cupcakes so that she could help me. She loved to crack the eggs and pour the ingredients in. The beaters were her favorite thing to do. Years later, as a college sophomore, she called me one day from Texas A & M and asked if she could come for an old-fashioned weekend of sitting on the counter, making cupcakes or cookies, and staying up to watch Jeopardy. We would let her stay up later than her brothers when we babysat so that we could watch the taped Jeopardy together. I was so touched that she wanted to come for the week-end. That's my "EM"!

When she was about five, I took her shopping. We found a beautiful red London Fog coat. I looked at the price tag and she asked me, "Gannie, is it too 'pensive'?" Needless to say, I bought that coat. She remembers it till this day. I pray that I will be able to take her little daughter shopping someday!

Emily graduated from Texas A & M and ended up moving to Washington D.C. to work for a Congressman. She met Jesse Lashbrook, a Texas boy, fell in love and married Jesse 5 years ago. We are so blessed to have Jesse in our family. An added bonus is to know his wonderful parents Jean and Don Lashbrook. Em and Jesse presented us with our precious great-granddaughter Landry Grace May 1, 2013. I have no doubt that little Landry Grace will be sitting on the countertop helping her Grandma Bella (my daughter Tara) make cupcakes very soon. Who knows, maybe I will get that opportunity on one of their visits to Gannie's! (Emily named me Gannie!) After 5 years in D.C. they are now living in Houston, Texas, where Landry's little brother Levi was born on July 7, 2014. I can hardly wait to spoil them both! My way of spoiling is to just pour on all the love I have!

Emily was not quite two years old when Adam Joseph was born. We rejoiced again. I again flew to LA to help Tara with both children. There is nothing like being a grandmother and watching your own child parent. We are so blessed!

Adam was about one year old when Tara and Joe moved back to Texas. Joe got a job in Tyler just two hours from Dallas. We were so happy to have them living two hours away. We got to see them often. I remember that Christmas noticing that Adam often bumped into things. Tara thought that he was clumsy. When he walked right into the ironing board, a horrible thought popped into my head. I thought, "Oh! No! Adam has a brain tumor and is going blind!" I dismissed that thought but suggested to Tara that she watch him carefully and that it might be a good idea to take him to get his eyes checked.

Shortly after that Adam would all of a sudden cry out in pain until he fell asleep. So Tara made an appointment with her Pediatrician, who also suggested that she take Adam to an Ophthalmologist. The eye doctor had no patience with this baby and told Tara to take him home, put the drops in his eyes and then return. Tara called me to ask me to find a Pediatric Ophthalmologist in Dallas. She could not get an appointment for more than a month. Then the doctor had a family emergency for which he had to fly out of town. It would be another month by the time Adam got in to be tested. The doctor did not like the paleness of the optic nerve and sent Adam for an MRI exam. The results were devastating. Adam did indeed have a brain tumor the size of a small grapefruit in that precious little head. The tumor, which was sitting on the optic nerve, caused blindness in the left eye with only tunnel vision in the right eye. Diagnosis – legally blind!

The next step was to see a brain surgeon and schedule surgery. I spread the word for prayers for Adam. That June morning our family gathered at the hospital waiting room. We prayed together. It was one of the longest days of our lives. Eight and one- half hours later the surgeon came out to tell us that Adam had come through the surgery just fine. Then he lowered the boom by telling us that the tumor (craniopharyngioma) had destroyed the pituitary gland, which is the major switch in the brain that regulates every hormone needed to sustain life. Adam would need to take meds all of his life so that he could live and function. He would need growth hormone shots or he would not grow. He would need the hormones that regulate the other major organs in the body. We were devastated, yet relieved that, first of all, Adam had made it through the surgery and secondly, that at least there was help available so that he could live.

Once Adam came out of ICU we all took hospital shifts so that he would never be alone. It was so painful to see him with a huge helmet-like bandage on his little head. He would cry out when the nurse came in or the med tech frequently drew blood. All we could do was pray for God's mercy on this precious baby and comfort him as much as we could. He loved the song "Jesus Loves Me" so one day when he was crying, I started singing it. He calmed down. There was a Jewish child next to him and the Rabbi and the parents were standing by his bed. I felt the need to explain to them that the song calmed Adam and was not intended in any way to offend them.

Bob was sitting with Adam one afternoon when Adam had a seizure, threw up, and was choking with the oxygen mask on. That was even more reason why we knew that one of us had to sit with him at all times. Chris and Danene drove down from Tulsa for a week to help out. We were also babysitting Emily as well. We helped Tara and Joe as much as possible. They could not stay at the hospital 24/7. I don't remember who walked into Adam's room after two weeks when Adam was standing up in bed and saying, "Get me out of this place!" What a joy!

His speech had not been affected at all. He was very verbal! All of us spent a lot of time on our knees during that time. God supplied the help we needed!

Adam continued to have frequent seizures. I would go to Tyler to take care of Emily while Tara and Joe were at the hospital with Adam. Adam was around four years old when we had been babysitting for a week while Tara & Joe were out of the country. He always woke up early. This particular Sunday morning he was sleeping later than usual, so I went in to check on him. He was having a seizure. I touched his face and realized that he was burning up with fever. Bob stayed with Emily while Arden, who was Greg's wife at the time and very pregnant, held Adam in the back seat while I drove down the freeway doing 80. Arden was a nurse at the hospital and called ahead to the ER to tell them we were coming in. Adam kept having seizures – about 20 or more that day. I felt so powerless and so concerned. Finally he was taken to ICU. Tara and Joe had left St. Thomas Island that morning to fly to Miami, then fly back to Dallas. There was no way for me to get in touch with them. There were no cell phones in those days. I met them at the airport that evening. Tara took one look at me and asked what was wrong. I broke the news that Adam was in ICU. I took them straight to the hospital. It had been a really long and trying day.

The doctor told Tara and Joe that there was a possibility that all the seizures could have caused brain damage. I came home totally exhausted but could not sleep. I prayed all night. The phone rang about 6:30 a.m. Joe said to me, "Gannie, somebody wants to talk to you!" I heard this precious little voice say, "Hi, Gannie, I am OK!" I could not hold back the tears of relief and tears of thanksgiving! Once again, my Lord came through! All I could say was, "Thank you, Lord!"

A few months later we had both Emily and Adam for the week-end. Adam woke up about 5:30 a.m. – the middle of the night for me. I was asleep but woke up with the sense that somebody was staring at me. It was Adam standing by my bed and whispering, "Gannie, can I have some oatmeal now?" I told him it was too early and that he could crawl into our bed and sleep some more. Again I felt the staring and opened my eyes to see Adam as wide awake as he could be, asking me if it was time to have breakfast yet. I gave in, got out of bed and fixed his oatmeal. I was so sleepy and was resting my tired head on my arm at the table, when Adam said, "Gannie, I just love coming to your house!" How could I possibly be upset with this precious little boy!

Adam had seizures quite often in school. In first grade he spent a lot of time in the nurse's office. His classmates, who were too young to understand what was happening, were frightened when he had seizures. He was called "retarded, weird, etc." One incident that speaks to Adam's wonderful attitude occurred when he went up to a little girl on the playground to ask her to play with him and she said, "No way, you are retarded!" Adam said, "That's OK, I will go find someone else to play with me!" Adam had and still has the most wonderful attitude about life. He was like a refreshing spring breeze blowing in wherever he went. He still is at 28 years old! I credit Tara and Joe's attitude plus God's grace!

Adam is currently working on his Master's Degree in Education. He continues to take all the meds necessary to keep him alive. In September of 2013 he married the love of his life Melissa Rishel, who graduated from Texas A & M this past June. She is now a Licensed Veterinarian Tech and is a surgical assistant to a Vet in Tyler. Adam and Melissa spent most of their first year of marriage apart since she was at school in College Station and Adam's job was in Tyler. They are so happy to be together every day now. We prayed for a special girl to come into his life and God heard our prayers. Melissa is that special girl who has blessed Adam and blessed our family abundantly. Adam is doing a terrific job at a Cable Company where he is employed as a troubleshooter! We have an awesome God who pours out His love and His blessings daily!

Alexander was born five years later. I drove to Tyler to take care of Emily and Adam, then Tara and the baby when they came home. This was Tara's third C-section. Alex had recovered nicely from major surgery when he was four hours old so we were grateful to God. My pet name for him is "My Velcro Baby." We were babysitting while Tara and Joe were on their annual company trip. Alexander was less than two years old and was clinging to me every day. When Tara and Joe returned, I met them at a restaurant on the highway so that they could take the three children back to Tyler. When I handed Alexander over to Joe, he cried and wrapped his little arms around me. He wanted to stay with me. That is how he got his name. He was clinging to me like Velcro. Joe peeled him away from me. I cried on the way home. Alex and I had really bonded. I was so touched by his love!

I mentioned to Alex that I might have to stop calling him "My Velcro Baby" once he has a girlfriend so as not to embarrass him. He said that if she were to be embarrassed by his pet name, then she would have to go. He said he would always be "My Velcro Baby." Alex is 24 years old now and a 2013 graduate of University of Texas at Tyler. His pet name will go on and on as long as I am around! My hard-working grandson was hired by Enterprise in their management training program right after his graduation. He is now an Assistant Manager after one year. We are so proud of the man he has become! My grandchildren and great-grandchildren bless me so abundantly! A part of me will live on and on! God has blessed me so very much!

Christopher Michael was born September 20, 1956, when Tara was 13 months old. From the very beginning Chris was a very easy-going and laid back child. His feedings took forever as he would coo and smile at me as the milk ran down his chin. I loved it except at the 2:00 a.m. feedings. He loved his big sister and followed her all around as soon as he could crawl and walk. He did everything she told him to do even when it got him in trouble. He missed her when she started Kindergarten. One morning when Chris and Lisa were playing in the backyard while Tara was at school, the next door neighbor gave them a cookie and Chris broke his in half so he could give Tara half when she came home. Their relationship continues to be close to this day.

Chris showed interest in fixing things at a very early age. One of the kids had tried to sharpen a crayon in our pencil sharpener and the crayon broke off. I tried to dig it out but failed. Chris was five years old at the time. He carefully took the pencil sharpener apart, cleaned it out and put it back together again. That was the beginning. When he was 17 years old he completely tore down his Mustang engine in our garage. I had never seen so many parts, nuts, bolts, screws, etc. I remember thinking to myself, "How is this boy going to know where these parts go?" Well, lo and behold, he rebuilt that engine and it worked! There were a few bits and pieces left over, but apparently they were not needed. Chris can fix anything and build anything. Today his hobby is restoring rusted out Mustangs and turning them into beautiful cars. To think it all started with a pencil sharpener!

Chris also loved animals. I do, too! However, my love does not extend to snakes I must say. It was Good Friday when I told the kids we all had to get ready for services. I went back to the bedroom to get ready and when I came out, no one was in the house. I walked to the kitchen and looked out of the window to see Bob and the four kids looking around our garage. They all had a terrible look on their faces when I asked them what they were doing. One of them said, "We are looking for Chris' snake. It got out!" My station wagon was parked in that garage so all I could think about was the possibility that I would get into my car and a snake would crawl across my feet while I died of a heart attack right then and there! Chris had been told that he could not have snakes for pets. We had gerbils, rabbits, hamsters, dogs, seahorses, fish, a domesticated white rat, even baby mink, an armadillo briefly, our dog Brandy, and Lisa's pet Spunky, the de-scented skunk, but I definitely drew the line at snakes.

Needless to say, I was very upset. We had to get to church, so the search was suspended and would continue once we got home. I have to tell you that I knelt down in church and told Jesus how angry I was with my son and asked for the grace not to kill him with words. We never did find that large snake, but every time I went out to the garage and especially when I got into my car, I was scared to death that it would appear.

When Chris was 13 and Lisa was 11, they wanted to buy a horse. We told them that they would have to have jobs to first of all, buy the horse, and second of all, pay for the upkeep. They decided that a paper route would be the way to do both. The only problem with the paper route was that Bob had to drive down to the corner on Sunday mornings, pick up the newspapers, come home, wake the kids up at 3:30 a.m., help them fold the papers, and drive them around to throw the papers. During the week, they rode their bikes to deliver the afternoon papers except on rainy, cold, icy, or snowy days. That was my job after teaching all day. So, the paper route was a family affair!

The day came to purchase the horse after Chris and Lisa had saved their money, $175 to be exact. Bob rented a trailer and drove them to pick up a Palomino named Tony. Tony had lived in a pasture for a few years so he was not the prettiest horse. They stopped by the house to introduce me to Tony. They were beaming and said to me, "Mom, isn't he beautiful?" Beautiful he was not. His coat was awful and his ribs were showing. He could have used some weight. I was thinking, "How could Bob have let them buy this mangy looking horse!" But I could not put a pin in their balloon of excitement. I simply smiled and nodded. They were both so happy!

They had rented space in a barn not too far from the house. They told me that I could not come down to see Tony until they had fattened him up and taken care of his coat. Three months went by before I was invited to see Tony again. I could not believe he was the same horse. He had a beautiful blond shiny coat. He had meat on his bones and was indeed a beautiful horse.

Chris and Lisa took turns showing him in horse shows. They did win some ribbons. The people at the barn helped the kids train Tony and learn how to ride in shows. Being responsible for taking care of a horse physically and financially taught them valuable lessons that I don't think we could have taught them.

Chris was among the youngest in his classes since the cut-off for school was December 31st in Louisiana and September 1st in Texas. We moved here when he was going into 3rd grade. I asked that he be kept back because of his age, but was told he was too bright to be held back. He was always the smallest in his classes and was bullied. He did well academically until his Sophomore year at Jesuit when he was introduced to pot. His grades suffered. In April of his junior year he left Jesuit and home, enrolled in Turner High School and moved in with a friend and his family. We were so distressed. He could not follow our family rules, which he admitted were not harsh or unusual. He wanted to be free to come and go as he wished and to stay out all night if he wanted to. We had to give him a choice, follow the rules and suffer the consequences when they were broken or not live at home. It was a tough decision but a necessary one. We could not allow him to do as he wished when the other three children followed our rules. We were broken-hearted that he chose to leave. He graduated with decent grades and because he had spent almost three years at Jesuit, he had more credits than necessary. He did not even know that we were at his graduation. We chased him across the stadium so we could give him a graduation present and let him know that we were there and that we loved him.

The next few years were tough for all of us. Chris was in and out of our lives. Sometimes we did not know where he was living. When we were going to celebrate our 25th Wedding Anniversary, Lisa drove in and out of parking lots in the area apartment complexes so she could find Chris. At the church when we were about to begin the ceremony to renew our vows, Chris surprised us by walking in with a tux on and a haircut. Lisa had found him and told him he had to come to our celebration. We were all so happy to see him. Not too long after that Chris went home to his apartment only to find his 21 year-old roommate hanging from a door. The young man had married out of high school because his girlfriend became pregnant. They had a car wreck when the baby was a few months old and both his wife and the baby were killed. He had never recovered from their deaths. Chris would bring him over for Sunday dinner sometimes. He was so depressed and so sad. Our hearts went out to him.

Chris called us that day to tell us what had happened. He was quite shaken up by such a tragic event. We were as well. I asked him if he wanted to come home to spend the night but he declined. It was the beginning of a big change in Chris.

Chris eventually moved back home. He was 24 years old and had lost his job. He also was kicked out of his apartment because he could not pay the rent. He showed up at the house one afternoon. He told me he had been living in his car and eating peanuts for 3 days until he got up enough courage to ask to move home until he got a job. Of course, we welcomed the prodigal son home with open arms. He managed to follow the rules for the most part.

My mother had had two heart attacks in 10 days and was in ICU. I had planned to visit her on Thursday of that week. I reminded Chris of the importance of letting me know where he would be and how to reach him. Of course there were no cell phones in those days. Well, I received the phone call at 6:30 a.m. on that Wednesday that my mother had died. I called his friend Danny, who was going to let Chris know so that he could call home. We got a flight to New Orleans that evening. Tara and Joe were flying in on Friday evening so I asked Joe to get a ticket for Chris if he got in touch with him. Chris ended up flying to New Orleans with Tara and Joe. Needless to say I was very angry and very hurt. Chris was close to his grandmother. I wondered how he would feel missing her funeral and I wondered how I would explain to my family that Chris wasn't there.

I was pleased that he made it but so angry with him that I could not really talk. All I could say to him was that we would discuss this later. Bob's parents and the rest of my family knew nothing about Chris being in and out of our lives for years. My grief was multiplied for my mother and my son.

We began to see a change in Chris. He turned his life around. He finally got a decent job and moved into an apartment. He designed and built the burners that burn natural gas off the oil wells. Then his boss decided to move the company to Tulsa, Oklahoma. I remember well the morning Chris came by in the U-Haul-It truck to say good-bye. My heart sank as he drove away. We had finally gotten our son back and now he was moving to Tulsa. Letting go once again felt like a mixed blessing. We were happy that Chris had a good job but sad that we would not see him for Sunday dinners, a big tradition in our family.

Chris met Danene Hasz in Tulsa. He brought her home on one of his week-end visits. He told us that if she were older, he would propose. At 19 she was 10 years his junior. We liked her from the start. Chris really fell in love and within a year they were married. Michael was born less than a year later. Then 13 months later Matthew was born. Chris and Danene had bought their first house. Life was going well for them. Then the bottom fell out in the oil business and Chris' company folded. He scrambled to find a job along with thousands of others looking for jobs. After months of doing odd jobs and struggling to support his little family, he got a job working for Mueller, where he designed and supervised the building of stainless steel equipment for pharmaceutical companies, hospitals and dairies. Mueller was in Springfield, Missouri, so Chris, Danene and the boys moved from Tulsa. Danene was a dental assistant to an Orthodontist for a few years, then became certified as a Neuro-Massage Therapist. She blesses her clients with her healing hands. She has blessed our family since the beginning in so many ways. Her parents Carol and Gary Hasz are a blessing as well! We are so grateful that Danene is doing so well since her thyroid cancer treatment 8 years ago.

After many years at Mueller, Chris got a job in Sharpsville, Pennsylvania in 2013. We were excited that he would be doing what he liked and at a salary commensurate with his abilities, but at the same time we were sad that they would be so far from home. Chris suffered a lot in his early years, but as Henry Nouwen said, "As we are healed, we become healers." Chris has been very involved in his church wherever he lived. He plays the guitar in the music ministry and teaches Bible studies. He is a wonderful example of a dedicated and beautiful Christian son, husband, father, grandfather and friend. He blesses us with his love and his wisdom. Again he is an example of how God takes all of our broken pieces and with His love makes us whole. He has been able to help many people in his 58 years because he has walked the walk!

Twenty-eight year old Michael has been in the Air Force for the past 10 years. For several years Michael kept the satellites in repair via the computer and now does Special Ops work. In December of 2013 he married Becca McGonagill. They live in New Mexico. Becca is an LPN and hopes to graduate from Nursing School by the end of 2015. They are a precious couple.

Twenty-seven year old Matthew married Rebecca Stewart in June of 2009. They gave us our precious little great-granddaughters, five- year-old Jessica and two-year-old Faith Elizabeth. They live in Tulsa. Matt is a licensed electrician and works for his uncle, his mother's brother, in his pool business. Rebecca is the Administrative Assistant to the Pastor at her church. We don't get to see them too often but when we do, it is a joyous occasion. Chris and Danene are so proud of their sons and so delighted to be grandparents and I am so proud of my grandsons and so happy to be a great-grandmother!

I will pick up Lisa's story with her struggle to get through school. She worked so hard in school but it was very difficult for her to do well. I remember her asking me when she was in fifth grade if she needed to know Math to be a mother. We were in the kitchen while I was cooking. Lisa always struggled with Math and Reading Comprehension. I told her that I would teach her how to measure ingredients and that she would be a successful cook. It broke my heart to think that she was worried that she would not be able to cook because Math was so hard for her. I did teach her to cook, something she does extremely well!

Lisa decided that college would be too hard for her so she got a job after she finished high school. She has always worked very hard and conscientiously at whatever she did. During this time I was in graduate school. At one of my graduations Lisa told me that she would love to get a college degree but that she did not think she was smart enough. I told her that she was smart enough and that if she wanted a degree, I would help her. She came home from work one day and told us that she wanted to be a Paralegal and was thinking of enrolling in El Centro Junior College to earn an Associates Degree. My first thought was, "Oh! But she will have to summarize 500 page briefs, etc!" But I did not say that to her. Lisa did enroll in the program and ended up graduating with a 3.6 GPA in 1987.

She was hired by the City of Dallas Attorney's Office and has been there 27 years. She has been the Senior Paralegal for several years now.

Then a few years later, Lisa decided that she wanted a Bachelor's Degree. So we encouraged her to go for it. She enrolled in the University of North Texas and while working full-time, managed to get her Bachelor of Arts Degree with a Minor in Emergency Management in 1997. Her GPA was 3.7 – quite an accomplishment for someone who struggled through grade school and high school. Lisa bought her first house and managed to pay for it in 15 years. She had horses until her last horse Chip died in 1996. She always demonstrated her strong work ethic beginning with getting the paper route with Chris when she was 11 years old. She was named "Outstanding Paper Carrier" by the *Dallas Times Herald* and always managed to balance her monthly bill. Not too shabby for a child who struggled in Math, huh!!!!

We had a terrible scare in 1995 when Lisa was having falls and other symptoms and the doctor thought she might have MS. We had a very trying week as we were praying and waiting to get a diagnosis. God came through again when the spinal tap was negative for MS. Her symptoms went away. At the time she was working full-time and going to school. We were so relieved and so grateful to God for answering our prayers once again!

Lisa met Paul Kupersmith when he had a one-time date with her room-mate. They became friends for several years. Paul's parents were deceased and his five siblings and their families lived in Missouri, so he spent holiday dinners with us. My children always brought home friends who had no place to go on holidays. When Paul had a stroke when he was 39, Lisa was there to help him recover. We wondered if the relationship would develop into more than a friendship, but it was 12 years later when we finally saw the relationship turn into more than just friends. Paul was facing some serious health problems since he had been diagnosed with a blood disor-der that throws clots (Anti Thrombin3 Protein S Deficiency) – whew! A mouth full, huh! They had fallen in love and were married on March 4, 2006. They had a one-day "honeymoon." Then Paul checked into the hospital for major exploratory surgery. That was the first of many hospital stays, which included gallbladder surgery, hernia surgery, pacemaker and defibrillator surgery. It was determined that Paul would need a heart and liver transplant back then, but because of his blood disorder, he was not put on the transplant list.

A year later they were on their way to the hospital for a procedure when Paul hemorrhaged when the varices in his esophagus ruptured. Paul was in a coma for several days. We were told that he had about three months to live and that he would never work again. Six weeks later Paul was back at American Airlines in his job as an airline mechanic. Once again the power of prayer was confirmed. That was in March of 2007. Paul was on his way to work one morning on I35 when his heart stopped and he crossed over three lanes without hitting a car or being hit by one in the morning rush hour traffic. He hit the concrete abutment, totaled his truck, and walked away with a scratch and broken glasses. Did he not have angels watching over him?????? Then a couple of years later he was on his way to work on a country road when his heart stopped again. He did not make the curve in the road and ended up hitting a tree head-on. Again he walked away with a few scratches and bruises. The saga continued as Paul had episodes of blacking out due to his heart stopping until the defibrillator could kick in. Lisa lived in constant fear that she would come home one day and find him dead.

Paul had an amazing attitude that got him through all the trauma he experienced. He kept going. He and Lisa traveled a lot and made the most out of life. Then on March 9, 2014, they were coming from their usual Saturday morning breakfast at I-Hop when Paul said that he did not feel well. Fortunately, Lisa was driving, so she pulled over just as Paul started hemorrhaging from the esophagus. She called 911 and they arrived in less than five minutes to rush Paul to the hospital. All the varices in his esophagus had ruptured again, but this time the doctors were not able to stop the bleeding. Paul went into a coma. Two days later the docs told Lisa that there was no hope for recovery. Paul had had a stroke on top of the bleeding. Lisa was told to make a decision about the life support measures Paul was on. His siblings had arrived from out of state so they all sat down with Lisa to make the decision. She called us to tell us that Paul had told her many times that he did not want to be kept on life support and since there was no hope for recovery, she made the decision to remove life support. On Tuesday morning, March 11, 2014, the whole family went up to the hospital to say our good-byes. Paul was in a deep coma but we were hoping that he could hear us tell him how much we loved him. At 2:30 p.m. life support was removed. Paul took his last breath at 4:17 p.m. The most difficult part of the day for me was watching the pain and suffering my daughter was going through. She and Paul had been best friends for so many years before their 8 year marriage and now her best friend and the love of her life was gone. As a Mom, I want to clean my children's wounds, put band-aids on them, kiss them and send them out to play. All I could do at that moment was hold Lisa and cry with her.

Paul's family was a wonderful support to Lisa. They are a close-knit family and were so gracious about making Lisa a part of their family. We are so grateful for the Kupersmiths. We all miss Paul so very much. It has been over a year and I sometimes still think Paul will walk through the door on Wednesdays. After Paul retired in December, 2013, he spent Wednesdays coming over to help me do odds and ends. Then Lisa would come over after work and we would all go out to eat. We treasure the times we spent with Paul and so appreciated his love for Lisa and for us. Paul often told me that I was his favorite mother-in-law! He had quite a sense of humor! We were blessed to have him for seven years longer than we were told. God is good!!!

Lisa joined a Grief Support Group and is doing well as she grieves her loss. She understands loss because she has had her share of loss in her life. She plans to retire from her job as lead paralegal with the Dallas City Attorney's Office in probably three more years. She recently bought some land to fulfill her heart desire to have a place where she can have a barn and horses and other animals. Lisa is a wonderful daughter, sister, aunt, sister-in-law to all of us. I am so grateful to God for allowing her to live for the first ten and one-half years with a condition that is usually fatal at birth. God has blessed us so abundantly! AMEN!

Greg was just 22 months old when we were transferred to Dallas. That precious baby was so confused as we were in one motel for two days and then another for eight days before our furniture arrived and we could move into our rented house. Every time we got into the car he cried to go home meaning the New Orleans home! He could unlock doors and climb fences like a monkey, so I was constantly on my guard! He really kept me on my toes. He wanted to do whatever his older siblings did – quite a challenge to protect him. After we moved from the rented house into our new home 10 months after coming to Dallas, Greg was straddling our new fence. When my neighbor asked him what he was doing on the fence, he replied, "I am concentrating on whether to climb over or not!" He ended up having over 100 splinters removed from his abdomen as he lay across Bob's lap. He did not attempt to go over the fence again.

Greg was reading labels in the Barber Shop when he was not quite four years old. The Barber was so impressed. I was hesitant to teach Greg to read for fear I might do it wrong, so when he would ask me, I would tell him that he would learn to read in Kindergarten. When I picked him up after his first day in Kindergarten, he appeared to be upset about something. I asked him what was wrong and he told me that he had not learned to read that day and I had told him he would when he went to Kindergarten. I should have been more specific. It wasn't long before he was reading books. School was easy for him.

Greg asked for drums when he was in 7th grade. He had been playing guitar at Mass since 5th grade. So, we relented and our house with filled with loud music with Chris on his bass and Greg on his drums. Lisa and Tara sometimes joined with their guitars. (Justice is served, though! Greg's son Forrest started playing drums in grade school. Chris's son Matt also became a drummer as well as a guitarist! Adam, Tara's son also plays drums! Serves them right, huh!)

Greg was in the Marching Band and the Jazz Band at Jesuit College Prep. Music has always been an important part of his life. He went to

Texas A & M but could not be in their Marching Band because only Corps members were allowed. He did not want to be in the Corps and commit four years to the military after graduation. However, he was the drummer for the Women's Chorus and in the Symphony Orchestra.

I remember the first Christmas that Greg had gone off to college. We had had a tradition of baking a birthday cake for Jesus and placing it under the Christmas tree since Tara was a baby. We would then sing "Happy Birthday" to Baby Jesus and blow out the candle. For some reason I thought that since the kids were all grown up that they might think it was a childish tradition. So, I did not bake my usual pound cake! Well, they were very upset that we did not have a birthday cake for Jesus. Sara Lee came to the rescue from my freezer. I thawed a pound cake in the microwave, stuck a candle in it and we had our usual tradition. I learned that day that you don't mess with family tradition in this family! Just 'cause Greg had gone off to college and the other kids were older did not mean that I should change our celebration of Christmas with a Baby Jesus Birthday Cake!!!!!!

Greg graduated with a degree in Agricultural Economics in 1985. From there he traveled with Up With People for a year. He traveled the U.S. and Europe and values that experience. His Up With People group was featured in the Super Bowl XX Half-time show in January, 1986, in the Superdome back in his birthplace of New Orleans. The camera was fixed on Greg playing drums for about 15 seconds. There was a lot of whooping and hollering at the Moulin household as we watched him on TV that day!

After returning home Greg got a job at American Airlines in their Reservation Department. He received several promotions and ended up in mid-management in the IT Department. He was with American for 21 years. During this time he met Arden Cronk, who was one of Adam's nurses when Adam had brain surgery. Arden and Greg were married the following spring in 1989. Kelsey Renee was born in November of 1991 and Forrest Gregory was born in June of 1993. Unfortunately, the marriage ended in 1999. Arden is still part of our family and is now married to

Jason Jacoby. Greg married Danita Littlefield in February, 2002. Danita is a precious addition to our family. "D" is an administrative assistant at a Pharmaceutical Logistics Company. She is also an expert in cake baking and decorating. (After one of my surgeries D called to check on me and asked me if there is anything I wanted to eat. I asked her if she and Greg would be going to a wedding anytime soon. She said "no." My family knows I have this thing for wedding cake and I was craving wedding cake in spite of having no appetite. The very next day Greg showed up with a small wedding cake. D had baked it for me. That's our D!) She is also a wonderful "Second Mom" to Kelsey and Forrest! As a side note, D had thyroid cancer in 2013 and is doing well. It is ironic that both daughters-in-law had thyroid cancer.

Because Greg has always been a "people person" he decided to change careers after he became certified as an EMT and a Paramedic. He had been on the bereavement team for American Airlines where he was sent to work with the families of those passengers lost in an airplane incident or crash. He spent four weeks in New York where he worked with families of the victims from the crash that happened shortly after 9/11. He realized that he wanted to be in public service, so he applied for a job at DFW Airport. The surrounding cities would not hire anyone over 35 and Greg was 45. He was hired by the Airport and went through the rigorous training as a firefighter since paramedics also have to be firefighters. He was valedictorian of his class. In 2013 he was promoted to Captain and is currently working on his Master's Degree in Emergency Management at OSU. I have always told my children that it is never too late to follow your dreams. They seem to have listened well!

Kelsey (23) received her CNA (Certified Nursing Assistant) her senior year in high school. She graduated early from high school and got a job working in a doctor's office where her Mom was the Nurse Practitioner. She started college and has been working full-time in hospitals on the night and evening shifts and going to school. She was recently hired by the doctor with whom her mother works so that she can spend evenings with Blake. She was going to get a Nursing Degree but is now thinking of perhaps teaching special education. Kelsey became engaged to Blake Martin a few months ago and married December 13, 2014.

Kelsey spent the night in my room in one of my hospital stays. She set her alarm for every one-half hour so she could wake up and check on me. She said she was a sound sleeper and did not want to miss my call for help. She was just a teenager then. This speaks to her tender and loving heart!

Forrest has the distinction of being "My favorite red-headed grandson." I told him that when he was three years old. He looked at me and said, "Gannie, I am your only red-headed grandson!" He still holds that title today at age 21. Forrest became interested in music at a very early age – must be in the genes. He started playing drums in grade school and became part of the Marching Band, the Symphonic Band and the Concert Band in both middle school and high school. He placed first in the State of Texas in drums and first in the Nation in drum competition. God blessed him with many talents and intelligence. He attended the University of Houston and was in their Marching Band. Then he took a year off from college to work full-time. He has been finishing his basics in Junior College and plans to enroll in the University of North Texas to major in sound engineering. In the meantime he was bitten by the love bug. He met Leticia Moura last winter while she was going to school here and working as an Au Pair. They fell in love, became engaged and married August 30, 2014, in Brazil. They will be living in Brazil until Leticia gets her Visa to return to the U.S. Forrest is continuing his education by doing on-line college courses this semester. Hopefully he and Leticia will be back in the U.S. by the spring semester of 2016. They are expecting Anna Gabriela at the end of July or early August. I hope she has red hair like her daddy!

One of the many things I love about my family is their willingness to help when there is a need or something I want. I started art classes in 2003. The only place I had to paint was the kitchen table, but at meal time I would have to put everything away so that we could eat. I did not have closet space for my art supplies, so my family decided that I needed an art studio. A plan was made to add a room to the den. Lisa took care of getting permits, people to do the slab and the frame, and what we would need. Chris, Danene and 16 year-old Matt came down from Springfield and along with Greg, D and Lisa began building the inside of my 20 x 22 art studio. Kelsey, who was 12 years old, learned how to tape and bed sheetrock. The City Inspector was very impressed with their work and remarked that he wished everybody took such pride in their work. The boys put in surround sound so I can enjoy music while I paint. They worked hard and had fun doing it! I enjoy painting on Sunday afternoons! What wonderful memories the studio holds of love and working together! I am a very blessed mother!

In addition to the studio the kids re-did our Master bath after my hip surgery and also re-did my kitchen after a major leak under the slab. Lisa recently re-did the guest bathroom after a major leak caused by foundation work. They have saved us thousands of dollars and have done professional jobs. They enjoy working together on projects!

God has blessed us so abundantly with our loving children, their spouses; our wonderful grandchildren, their spouses; and our precious great-grandchildren. The greatest blessing is that they love God, love one another and they love us. It doesn't get any better than this!

Chapter 13- Spiritual Direction

"Freeing The Chains That Bind"
by
Liz Moulin

Spiritual Direction Training & Retreat Work

§

"Whatever you undertake will go well and
light will shine on your path."

(*THE JERUSALEM BIBLE*, JOB 22:28)

THE NIGHT BEFORE GREG'S JESUIT graduation in June, 1981, I had a dream
that led me to where I am today. I dreamed that I walked into the office
of Father Elliott, the President of Jesuit College Prep at the time, and
he swung around in his chair to tell me that I needed to become a public
speaker and write a book. I have always been interested in dream work and
do believe that God speaks to us in dreams. (I spent 6 years in a Jungian
dream group for therapists.) What blew my mind was that the very next
day before the graduation ceremony an announcement was made that Fr.
Elliott had died the night before of a brain tumor – the same night that I
had had the dream. Now I really did not know Fr. Elliott that well having spoken to him briefly at Jesuit functions. I was stunned and asked
the Lord to show me what the dream meant. Was I supposed to become
a public speaker and how was that to happen? Was I supposed to write a
book and about what?

Shortly after the dream, which was just four months since breast cancer, I was asked to be a spokesperson for the American Cancer Society. I gave talks on dealing with breast cancer to nursing students and medical students. Around the same time I was asked to join the Inner Healing Ministry team at Mount Carmel Center, where I gave talks on spirituality. I have always been drawn to spirituality. So now I had become a public speaker.

I was also in graduate school at the time. One of my courses was Tests and Measurements where we had to learn the various tests given to children and adults. We also had to take the tests, such as IQ, Reading Scores, and Personality Tests. Our professor asked us to write a paper describing all of our scores in a creative way. I wrestled with the creative part and was inspired to write an allegory of my life by writing the process of the caterpillar becoming a chrysalis, then a butterfly. People who read it over the years encouraged me to have it printed. I sent it to a couple of publishers but was turned down, so I put it aside. I pulled it out in 2012, some 22 years after I wrote it and self-published and illustrated the book myself. So, now I had fulfilled that dream I had about Fr. Elliott. The dream continues, though! I am convinced more than ever that God speaks to us in our dreams!

I was asked to give talks, mini-retreats, days of reflection at my church. Doing so seemed to become natural to me. I really enjoyed writing my talks and giving them. I had found my niche! I loved teaching people about how to deepen their spiritual lives and come to know the Lord in a deeper way. I had been making retreats at Montserrat Jesuit Retreat House in Lake Dallas since 1970 and quickly adopted Ignatian Spirituality. The basic premise of this spirituality is finding God in all things, which has had a tremendous impact on my life. I find it very comforting to look for how God is working in every situation. I had had the Carmelite spirituality growing up with the Sisters of Mount Carmel in New Orleans and again at the Mount Carmel Center here in Dallas. So, my spiritual life was very rich with all of those influences.

I could fill a book with all of the wonderful ways God has blessed me on my retreats at Montserrat Jesuit Retreat Center in Lake Dallas, Texas, and at the Jesuit Spirituality Center in Grand Coteau, Louisiana. The one spiritual experience that I have been encouraged to share is when I was on retreat at Montserrat and my Retreat Director Fr. Joe McGill asked me what I would like to do for a penance after my confession with him. I told him that I needed to write a thank you to the Lord for my imperfections. I know that came right from my heart. So I went to my room and wrote the following – written 7/10/97:

Dear Lord,

I thank you for my weaknesses and my sinfulness because I have come to realize that owning them, not excusing them, embracing them, not beating myself up about them, but truly acknowledging them helps me to accept who I am in You. As long as I cling to my limitations I do not have room for You. As long as I focus on them, I cannot focus on You. As long as I beat myself up about them, I remain stuck in them. They have power over me. I give them the attention I need to be giving to You in my life. So, Lord, I thank You for allowing me to see how I have been looking at the dark areas and trying to control them, then failing miserably and condemning myself. How can I experience Your presence within when my container is so filled with me and all my junk – my sinfulness, my limitations? Lord, please help me to empty my container of me so You can enter it! Please help me to let go of "ME" so I can find "ME" in YOU! Help me to trust that You love me just as I am and that I don't have to be perfect to be loved by You. I am loved by You because You called me by name and I am Yours. O, Lord! My soul is thirsting for You! Please come into the emptiness – the loneliness. I long for your presence, O Lord!

Thank you, Lord, for Your wisdom and grace to look at the "real me" and to be grateful that You created the "real me" in the splendor of all my sinfulness and limitations. I rejoice in my weaknesses, I give You the whip I've used to beat myself up. I think of how You were scourged with a whip just for me and my sins. I know I insult You when I scourge myself. Please forgive me, O Lord! Forgive me for doubting Your immense love for me? I love you, Lord! Liz

In 1998 when insurance companies were making it difficult to collect payments for therapy, my practice along with every therapist, began to drop. I was praying about where God wanted to lead me when I received a brochure in the mail that Fr. Bill Jarema from the Mercy Center in Colorado Springs would be coming to Montserrat to do a year's training in Spiritual Direction. I had trained with Fr. Sam Anthony Morello at the Mount Carmel Center back in the early 80's, but had to devote most of my time to building my therapy practice then. So, I enrolled in the year's training. About the same time I was invited by Fr. George Wiltz (my first date when we were sixteen!) to begin giving retreats at Montserrat and to join an Ignatian Spirituality Training Group. God opened the doors for me. I also gave some of the training to our Montserrat Group. I felt so at home! The story goes on!

In 2009 the Director of Spiritual Formation at SMU's Perkins School of Theology, Reverend Dr. Fred Schmidt, asked Fr. Joe Tetlow and me to teach in their Spiritual Directors' Training Program. I also had been in Fr. Joe's Ignatian Spirituality Training classes. We had done several workshops together. Fr. Joe was transferred to St. Louis two years ago, so I have been teaching the class alone. It has been almost six years of wonderful classes. What thrills me most is that most of my students are Protestant Ministers, Episcopal priests, and lay ministers getting certified in spiritual direction. God is truly working among His people! My hope and prayer is that I can continue to teach for a few more years even though I just celebrated my 80th birthday. To think it all started with a dream!!!!!! God is awesome!!!!!!!

After much prayer and discernment I recently gave up doing three-day retreats at Montserrat. I find that I can no longer do 12-hour days.

However, I will give mini-retreats of one day at a time. I gave up doing therapy two years ago but still do work for the Dallas Diocesan Marriage Tribunal which entails interviewing people seeking an annulment and those who are planning to remarry after an annulment. I will continue to see my directees as long as I am able. The minute I don't know why the person is sitting in front of me or why I am here will be the minute I have to fold up my tent. I pray that never happens!

This past October I taught a four Saturday class at Montserrat on "Praying the Ignatian Way." I am part of the Ignatian Spirituality Institute, where classes are provided on Saturdays from September through May. Teaching is one of my passions. I am so grateful that God has called me to this wonderful ministry. I remember so well playing the role of a teacher to my dolls when I was very young. The seed must have been planted at an early age! God is awesome!

I just co-authored another book with my dear therapist friend Linda Carmicle. It is called *The Psychotherapy of Wholeness: A Comparison of Redecision Therapy and the Ignatian Spiritual Exercises.* It is hot off the press as I write. Hopefully these Memoirs I am currently writing will be published in 2015. I have another book in mind and pray I can write it next year. I have come a long way since that 17 year old who did not think she was smart enough to go to college! Thanks be to God! He did not give up on me! He has blessed me so abundantly!

Chapter 14 - My Spiritual Journey

My Spiritual Journey

§

"I know the plans I have in mind for you – it is Yahweh who
speaks – plans for peace, not disaster, reserving a future
full of hope for you. Then when you call to me, and come
to plead with me, I will listen to you. When you seek me
you shall find me, when you seek me with all your heart;
I will let you find me (-it is Yahweh who speaks…)

(*THE JERUSALEM BIBLE*, JEREMIAH 29:11-14)"

WHEN I THINK OF MY spiritual journey, I cannot help but be in awe of how
God has called me into a deeper relationship with Him since that first
experience at Mass when I was only five years old. I have always been curi-
ous about everything and yearned to know more and more. That hunger
to know God and be in relationship with Him has grown and grown as
the years rolled by. I have always been drawn to spirituality, for which I
am eternally grateful. When I look back on all the trials and tribulations
of my life, I can see how that spirituality comforted me and encouraged
me to keep going. The times when I thought I could not cope anymore,
God's grace pulled me out of the depths of discouragement to give me
hope. One of my favorite sayings is, "This, too, shall pass!"

One of my purposes in writing my Memoirs was to give hope to others
who are going through tough times and feeling all alone. There have been

so many people who encouraged me and supported me throughout my journey. That reminds me of one of the sayings from my Mentor Father Sam Anthony Morello, OCD, who would say, "What we are all about is the Body healing the Body!" The very first time he said that to me I asked him to explain what he meant. He said that we are all members of the Body of Christ and we are called to participate in healing the Body of Christ. That is our mission!

I have experienced that healing over and over again by the people in my life. Sometimes the person was a stranger, yet I was touched by something he/she said or did. An example- I had gone to the cafeteria to eat lunch. That morning I had seen a couple in therapy and the session did not go well at all. The same thing had happened the day before. People often came for marital therapy when it was almost too late to resuscitate a dead marriage. As I sat there eating my lunch, I was wondering what a nice girl like me was doing in the midst of chaotic therapy. It was so difficult! Then I noticed an older couple a few tables away just staring at me. I had to walk by their table to exit the cafeteria and as I did the gentleman said to me, "Excuse me, Ma'am, but we wanted to tell you how lovely you look and how pretty you are!" The wife nodded in agreement. I smiled and thanked them, then went on my way feeling gratitude in my heart. That was God's way of loving me in my need to feel worthy.

It happened again on my 80th birthday. I had gone for bloodwork early that morning and stopped to get breakfast on my way to another appointment. As I sat eating my breakfast, the couple at the table across from me got up to leave. They walked over to me and the lady said, "Excuse me, but my husband and I were admiring how lovely you look and how pretty you look in that color." He nodded in agreement. I told them that they had made my day since I was celebrating my 80th birthday that day. Then the lady told me that they were on their way to the hospital for an MRI because the doctor thought her husband might have a brain tumor. She said that he had Alzheimer's and that she was hoping that the disease was the reason for his memory problems and not a brain tumor. I told her I would pray for him and for her. They smiled and left. What a lovely thing for them to do! I immediately started praying for them both. It is about the Body healing the Body! There have been multiple times over the years where God has touched my heart through another person.

The Ignatian premise of "Finding God in All Things" has certainly been a comfort and a gift to me for more than half of my life. I am constantly looking for how God is working in my life and the lives of others. I am so privileged to have been called to the ministry of Spiritual Direction and Retreat Work, where I can see firsthand how God is working in so many lives. I so enjoy training others to be Spiritual Directors. Henri Nouwen, one of my favorite spiritual writers, was right on target when he said, "As we are healed, we become healers!" The gift keeps on giving! Thanks be to God!

I am so grateful that I started making retreats at Montserrat Jesuit Retreat House in 1970. The Jesuits have been an important part of my spiritual formation for 45 years. I am also grateful to Fr. Sam Anthony Morello, who taught me meditation and contemplation in addition to the Jesuits. God is so good about placing people in our lives at just the right time.

One of the most profound meditation experiences I had at Mount Carmel Center with Fr. Morello is one that had really stayed with me for 32 years. Father read a story of an Indian Monk who had gone to the desert to pray for 40 days. He lived in a little grass hut during this time. As he was praying one day, the ground started shaking. He knew that a herd of animals was headed his way and that he could be trampled by them. So he got louder and louder with his prayers of praise to God. The herd of elephants went around the little grass hut and the Monk was saved from being crushed to death. Then Father asked us to go back into that scene and become the monk in the story and let God lead us where He would have us go. As I was kneeling in my little grass hut, I felt the ground shaking and the herd of elephants coming my way. I began to praise God very loudly and the herd went around the little hut. I heard a "thump, thump" right outside the little opening in the grass hut. I opened my eyes to see what it was and saw an elephant dancing to my praises. His trunk was in the opening and I saw Jesus standing there with a rope around the elephant's neck. In my heart I heard Him say, "Liz, make friends with your elephant!" He handed me the rope to hold. My elephant represented the previous year of so many trials and tribulations – Bob's loss of job, Chris finding his roommate hanged, my breast cancer, etc. I reached up to pet the elephant whom I named Iggy and told him that we would be friends from now on. Iggy goes with me everywhere. He represents all the big things in my life and God gives me the grace to embrace them in the form of my elephant. What a gift! I have enjoyed many spiritual insights and graces through meditation and contemplation!

I am so grateful that God gave me an active imagination!

I have experienced God's healing power so many times in my 80 years. Perhaps the most significant healing in me has taken place over the years as I have worked to overcome the tremendous shame I carried around since I can remember. I wrote earlier about the shame of having an alcoholic father and a mother who was a faith-healer and fortune teller. For most of my life I felt as though there was something intrinsically wrong with me. I remember asking my friends and my spiritual directors over the years to tell me what was wrong with me. My combined interest in psychology and spirituality has driven me to really know myself and to understand why I behave the way I do. Yet the dark cloud of shame hovered over me even after I really came to know and to believe that I am precious in His sight and loved as I am. For years I could list all my faults but had difficulty owning my gifts and all the good things I am as God created me and continues to create me anew each day!

My awareness of how carried shame impacts us so profoundly came about when I did training with Pia Mellody in Shame Reduction Work in the 80's. I had been a therapist for a few years and witnessed my clients getting better, yet I knew that something was still missing in the complete healing they sought. I felt the same way about myself. I had done a lot of work on my family of origin woundedness but kept searching for the missing piece of the puzzle. I found that missing piece in my training with Pia for three years. I was also in group therapy with Pia for a year. I learned the concept of carried feeling reality from her. Carried feeling reality is something all of us experience when the adults in our lives are not appropriate with their feeling reality when we are children. For instance, if a parent or both do not express feeling reality in a healthy manner, the children take it on. If a parent is either raging out of control in anger or stuffing the anger, it becomes an energy field that settles on the child. The same applies to fear, pain and shame. I like to describe it as a container that all children have. In a healthy family the container gets filled with love, acceptance and good values. If a parent(s) is not dealing with anger, fear, pain or shame appropriately, then the child's container gets filled up with these feelings that are carried until therapy extracts them someday. Expressing anger, fear, pain and shame appropriately does not harm the children but teaches them to also express feelings in a healthy manner. The very detrimental feeling reality of shame occurs when an adult abuses a child emotionally, intellectually, spiritually, physically or sexually because that adult is being shameless. The result is that the shame then settles on the child, thus the container gets filled with shame.

I don't want to re-write a book about the concept of carried feeling reality so I would suggest that you read Pia Mellody's book, *Facing Codependence*, to better understand the concept. Where I am going with this is to explain how carried shame impacts our lives by sharing how shame kept me in bondage for most of my life. I began to realize how the shame I was carrying impacted how I felt about myself as I learned about it from Pia and my own therapy. I did Shame Reduction work with Pia whereby I gave back the carried shame symbolically to my parents and to others who had shamed me through the years. It was very freeing to do this work. But somehow, though I felt better about myself, I would be thrown back into thinking that there was something wrong with me whenever I was put-down or shamed in any way about who I was.

A few examples of being thrown back into my shame core occurred when: When I was almost four years old, I was in the A & P Grocery Store in Gretna, Louisiana, with my parents, my sister and her husband.

We were ready to check out when I told my Mama I really had to go to the bathroom badly. She told me I had to wait until we got home. It would take twenty-five minutes for us to drive home. I pleaded with her to take me to the bathroom but was again told I had to wait. When we got into my brother-in-law's car, I had an accident. I was shamed by my Mama, my sister and my brother-in-law. When we got home, my Mama picked me up and put me in the bathtub with my shoes and soiled clothing still on. I remember feeling so ashamed and kept telling her, "But I told you I had to go badly!" as I sobbed uncontrollably.

Then when I was five years old my Daddy took me to the dentist for the first time. My front baby teeth had not fallen out yet but my second teeth were coming out behind them. The dentist pulled my baby teeth, pointed to what I thought was the floor and told me to spit. I did not know what the white bowl was for so I spit on the floor. He was upset because I did not spit in the white bowl. I was very upset and kept saying, "I didn't know!" I was always crushed when I thought I had done something wrong.

I have already written about the time I saved my mother's life when I was 7 years old. I cannot explain why I felt shame but I did. I suppose I took on my mother's shame.

I felt shame when my mother took me with her to make a nine- church novena so that my Daddy would die. It went against what I was taught in Religion class by the Nuns. I was very confused at the time. I just knew somehow that this was wrong to be doing.

I felt shame when my Daddy accused me of going to daily Mass to sleep with the priests. It was not my shame but his shame, but I did not understand why I felt so bad. Then I felt shame when the Monsignor kissed me when I was 13 and ostracized me from the pulpit though not by name. About that time I was shamed by my classmates when I had to step over their outstretched legs after Communion when they refused to move down. I was shamed often by being called "Goody, goody two shoes!"

I felt a lot of shame when my classmates excluded me from the carpool when I was a boarder at Mt. Carmel my sophomore year. I was convinced that there was something wrong with me then and when I was not invited to a slumber party but the girls had stopped by my house to get directions to the party. I kept getting the message that I was defective in some way.

As an adult I experienced feeling the same way when neighbors had a party and Bob and I were not invited. Again when we had applied to join a group at church but were not accepted. I could not help but wonder what was wrong with me. There were many others instances of being left out.

I experienced shame in graduate school. There was an unfamiliar term on a test question so I went up to the Professor's desk to ask him to define it for me. His answer was, "You are a graduate student, you should know what that means!" He would not tell me so I had to figure out what it meant. I felt shame again. In another class we were to take the test scores of a child with a learning disability and write a two-week curriculum to address his deficits in every subject. It meant a third of our grade in that course. So I spent a couple of week-ends working on the chart and took it to my Professor before class to be sure I was on the right track before I typed it up. He looked at it and told me I was on the right track – period! When we got to class, other grad students raised their hands to tell the prof that they did not know how to do this project. He then said, "Liz, you have done such a beautiful job on yours, tell the class how to do it!" So, I shared what I had done and then sat down. At the break one of my class-mates came up to me and said, "I will never be in another graduate class with you. I am sick and tired of you always setting the curve and always doing the best work. It makes all of us look bad!" I had to fight back tears as I sat in the second half of that class. To make matters worse we had to stand in line to receive a major paper at the end of that class. This student was right behind me. As Dr. W handed me my paper, he said, "Liz, this is one of the best graduate papers I have ever read!" I could feel K's eyes throwing daggers at me. Dr. W did not know what had transpired earlier. When I ordinarily would have driven home from TWU feeling great, this night I fought back tears. I kept thinking that my hard work had paid off yet I was feeling shame. Too bad I did not know about carried shame then. I was in my forties and so were most of my classmates. You would think that adults would be mature. I learned that age has nothing to do with maturity.

I somehow knew that more healing had to be done in me. Why did I continue to think that there was something wrong with me when I had not done anything wrong? The irony of it all was that I did not think I was smart enough even though the evidence proved otherwise.

As I was reflecting on other ways I was shamed, I realized that the Pediatrician who called me a neurotic mother had shamed me as well. Then there was the surgeon who admitted me to the hospital and scheduled gall bladder surgery without first doing x-rays then learned the night before that I did not have gallstones but had an ulcer. He told me not to read a medical book before I came to see him again. I was not the one who diagnosed me, he was, but he was blaming me. Needless to say I never went back to him. He was so angry with me when he should have been angry with himself for jumping to false conclusions before he did tests. I also react to false accusations. I had not read a medical book.

Because I had such a deep shame core, I took everything to heart and felt defective when someone gave me the message that I was defective in some way or I should not be who I was. My life started off with the injunction of "Don't BE" and continued with the injunction of "Don't be who you are!" I have come a long way in refuting those injunctions. A recent insight into shame seemed to complete my healing journey around shame. I was making my annual Directed Retreat at Monserrat when I shared a recent experience with someone whereby I got the message that there was something wrong with me. My Director and I began talking about the shame I felt about who I was and the sources of the shame core. I took the shame to prayer and realized that the shame core started in utero when the doctor said I was a tumor and my mother said it was her change of life. Now there is no way I would consciously know this as a fetus; however, I truly believe that the infant in utero picks up on the mother's feelings and what is going on with her. It made so much sense to me as I thought about all the clients I have worked with over the past 30 plus years. I cannot prove it but I know that I know that my shame core began before I was born. I prayed Psalm 139 and was comforted. My mother did not want me but God wanted me to be born. I felt a tremendous sense of healing deep within my being. A heavy burden seemed to be lifted. I experienced a freedom from my shame core. I now know at my deepest level that I am not defective, only perfectly imperfect and that is OK. I am so grateful to God!

In all of my years of being in the healing profession as therapist and spiritual director I realize more than ever how healing takes place in layers and in stages. In developing healthy boundaries many years ago and experiencing a lot of healing I managed to shake off any shaming experiences that occurred. What remained though was the question of what is wrong with me. It is so freeing to know that I am not defective but just a perfectly imperfect human being with her faults, sinfulness, gifts and talents. This is who I am in Christ Jesus! I give thanks to the Lord for His unconditional love and healing!

I share this experience with you to give you hope, to help you know you are loved and accepted by God, to show you how healing takes place, and to let you know that healing is a life-long process. Join me in giving God praise, thanks and glory!

Liz Moulin

Challenges - Stepping Out in Faith

§

"I promise that, ever hopeful, I will praise you more and
more, my lips shall proclaim your righteousness and power
to save, all day long. I will come in the power of Yahweh to
commemorate your righteousness, yours alone. God you
taught me when I was young, and I am still proclaiming your
marvels. Now that I am old and grey, God, do not desert me:
let me live to tell the rising generation about your strength
and power, about your heavenly righteousness, God."

(THE JERUSALEM BIBLE, PSALM 71:14-18)

IT WAS A WEDNESDAY NIGHT August 6, 2008, when I experienced chest
pain that wrapped around my right shoulder into my back. It was bedtime
so I thought I could lie down and ignore the pain till it went away or I
would fall asleep. Well, it did not go away and I could not fall asleep, so I
got up and told Bob that I thought we needed to go the hospital. (I might
interject here that I had prayed for the wisdom to know when to ignore
pain and when to check it out!) By the time we got there the pain had
subsided. Before we got out of the car I told Bob that we could go home
now since I felt better. He told me that he wanted to be sure I was OK and
so I needed to be checked out in the ER. I reluctantly got out of the car.
When I told the nurse that I had had chest pain, she immediately took me

back to a room. An EKG was performed and bloodwork was done. Then the doctor came in to tell me that I was not having a heart attack. I wanted to get out of there. The doctor then asked about my family history – my parents having heart disease; my two brothers dying of heart attacks suddenly at ages 50 and 52 just five months apart; my sister having major heart surgery at age 44; my remaining brother dying at age 64 just three years after quadruple bypass; and two nephews dying of heart attacks in their 40's along with several cousins; and a niece dying of a stroke. The doctor's eyes widened as he was about to discharge me, then he said, "I think we need to keep you tonight so we can run some tests tomorrow."

I was scheduled to have stents put in the next afternoon. Waiting all day without food was a real challenge. I was taken into the Cath Lab about three p.m. I had had at least four heart catheterizations before and was not put to sleep but this time I was out. I awoke to the doctor sighing as though he was frustrated. I said to him, "Are you having trouble?" I was immediately knocked out again. When I next woke up, I heard Lisa saying, "Get the nurse, Mom is having a stroke!" I was slurring my words and the left side of my face felt funny. I seem to remember hearing someone say when I was in recovery, "She's stroking!" It seems I was having a stroke. The doctor was called in then a Neurologist came in to test me. They agreed that I had stroked.

There was a discussion about putting me on Coumadin. The Cardiologist disagreed and recommended two Baby Aspirin a day instead. I was relieved with that decision. I did not want to take Coumadin. The Doctor who was sighing while trying to get the stents in was truly frustrated because the calcium deposits in my heart arteries were too hardened to allow the stents to go through. So a decision was made to do bypass the next day. I had not met the Doctor before nor did I see him after the failed attempted stent procedure.

The next morning a heart surgeon came into my room to introduce himself and to explain the bypass surgery. I was in shock by what had transpired. My speech had returned and I had no obvious problems from the stroke. Fortunately I was in the hospital when it happened so I was immediately given the right medication to prevent permanent damage from the stroke. It was late afternoon before I was taken to surgery. That morning my Pastor Fr. Michael Forge came to the hospital to give me the Sacrament of the Sick. Bob and I were so grateful to him. It was another long day for all of us. I had five major blockages that were bypassed with an artery from my left arm and a vein from my right thigh. The surgeon was able to take care of the blockages with a triple bypass. I spent a couple of days in CICU but did not remember it. I was brought to my room on Sunday and was happy to see my family. The next day the surgeon suggested that I needed a pacemaker so another surgeon was called in. He was planning to do the implantation that afternoon but when he lowered my bed to check me out, I became very nauseated. He then said that he could not possibly put in the pacemaker because of the nausea. I was relieved but scared. Why was all of this happening to me? It was all so fast and furious! I really did not want any part of it. I kept telling Jesus that and asking Him to get me through this horrible experience. That same day the nurse got me out of bed. I sat in a chair for about a half hour and asked to go back to bed. The pain was tolerable but I was very uncomfortable with my sternum cracked and wired back together with a ten inch incision down the middle of my chest. My arm also hurt with its eight inch incision where the artery was taken for the bypass as well as my thigh with its four inch incision where a vein was removed. I came home on the tenth day. One of the blessings in having bypass was that the surgeon was able to do an ablation for my A-Fib, which I had had for several years. There is a blessing in everything that happens to us.

Chris and Danene had come down from Springfield. It was decided that Danene would stay for a couple of weeks to help me since her job allowed her to take time off. Tara and Joe were living in Tyler at the time and Lisa was working full-time. Danene was a wonderful help. I could not bathe myself or wash my hair. She bathed me every day and helped me get dressed. I am usually the one helping another so I had to learn to receive help big time. It was also a lesson in humility. I came home with a drain in my chest. The amount of the fluid had to be drained several times a day and had to be down to a certain amount before the drain could come out. It took almost two weeks before I could get the drain out. I was really terrified of having it pulled out. Bob and Danene came into the examining room with me for support. Dr. P pulled the drain out before I realized it. I was amazed that it was pain free. What a relief!

I was having breathing problems and my back was really hurting. I had no appetite and was quite miserable. I could not lie down to sleep because I could not breathe. We went in to see the Cardiologist, who told me that this was normal after bypass. I told him that I had several friends who had had bypass and not one of them had trouble breathing. I could not walk across the floor without gasping for breath. I got no relief and felt as though the doctor was not hearing me. I was feeling so desolate and pleading with God every night to hear my prayer and give me relief. I went back to the cardiologist the following week when he did an echocardiogram. He said I had some fluid in my chest but not enough to cause a problem or to be drained. The breathing problems went on for several weeks. I became very depressed and very scared. I knew something was wrong but was being told it was normal to feel the way I did. I saw the surgeon again and he told me that there was not enough fluid to be causing the symptoms I was having. He diagnosed me with Pericarditis. He did not want to put me on Cortisone again so he prescribed Indocin. The second day of this drug I developed severe cramping and bleeding. Back to the hospital we went. The medication gave me colitis. The doctor wanted to keep me over night but I refused. I came home to recover. It was just another setback to deal with. I began to feel like Job!

The breathing problems continued. I was so discouraged. I also developed bed sores because I was sleeping sitting up in the lounge chair part of the sofa in the computer room. Bob would sleep in the other lounge part of the sofa and would hold my hand until I fell asleep. I cried out to God every night. "Where are you, Lord? Why are You not answering my cries for help? I cannot breathe! Am I dying, Lord?" Bob did his best to comfort me but I was beyond being comforted! It was terrifying to be struggling to get every breath! I knew in my head that God would not abandon me, yet I struggled to believe it as I gasped for every breath! I don't think I have ever felt such desolation in all of my life!

Since I was getting no help from the Cardiologist, I decided to find a new one. I also took it upon myself to see a Pulmonologist. I had seen Dr. Julye Carew before because of frequent bronchitis and pneumonia due to damage from radiation when I had breast cancer. She saved the day. She ended up draining five pounds of fluid from my chest. By this time it was over two months since bypass. What a relief! I could breathe easier and felt so much better for a few days. Then the breathing problems returned. An x-ray showed that the right lung had collapsed and that the fluid was back. I was so desolate when I was given the news and told that I would have to have lung surgery. Danene flew back to help take care of me again. A week later I had a six inch incision between two ribs in my back and again another tube draining my chest. I had difficulty breathing on my own after surgery so I was put on a ventilator. I ended up being in recovery till late that night. Bob and the kids were allowed to come into see me briefly. They waited all day until about 7 p.m. that night, then left to get some dinner and went home to wait for a phone call that I had finally been taken to a room. It was a miserable time for me and my family as well. I was so thirsty and so scared. They had finally taken me off the ventilator. I kept asking them when I could see my family again and the nurse kept telling me that I would get a room soon. I had had surgery at 7 a.m. that morning.

About 6 p.m. another lady was brought into the cubbyhole recovery room where I was. She had had gallbladder surgery and was nauseated. The nurses were busy focusing on her. Then she was taken to a room about 8:30 p.m. I asked when I could see my family and was told they had all gone home because it would be a while before my room was ready. I felt so frightened and so alone. I wanted to know why this lady got a room and I did not. I did not get a sufficient explanation. That day was one of the worse days since all of this began in August. It was now November and I was just worn out dealing with health issues. I felt totally abandoned by God and everyone.

Finally I was taken to a room by 10:00 p.m. I called home to tell them the room number. Danene said she would come over to spend the night with me. I was so grateful. I had been crying off and on all day. I was so miserable and so in need of comfort. It was a blessing to have Danene there with me all night. Surprisingly one of the drains was removed the next morning and I was sent home with the remaining drain. Again the fluid had to be down to a certain measurement before it could be removed. It was deja-vu all over again. The tube was in my back and wrapped around my lung up into the chest and around the top of the lung. I was so disappointed each day when the fluid levels were not coming down. Finally, after two weeks, Dr. P removed the tube.

Once again I was bathed and dressed for two weeks. Danene was wonderful. Right after she flew back home I got the flu, even though I had had a flu shot. I had 103 fever and was flattened. It seemed that all I could do was keep recovering from health issues. I was really beyond weary by this point. The first time Danene was here after bypass she was explaining to Bob how to bathe me and wash my hair. He told her not to worry, that he would just take me out to the driveway and hose me down. His wonderful sense of humor helped relieve many a tough time in my life!

My precious family decided that it was too difficult for me to get into the tub to take a shower, so Chris and Danene came down from Springfield for a couple of weeks, Greg and Lisa came over in the evenings and weekends and I ended up with a beautiful new shower and bathroom. It was a lot easier to walk into a shower rather than climbing over a tub! I have the most loving and giving family! There really is a blessing in everything!

As I began to recover from all the health crises in the past three months, my breathing improved. My energy level was very low, but I was encouraged that I was slowly getting better each week. Lisa and Paul brought meals over and Tara came in some week-ends to help out. My family really took over during the holidays. Thanksgiving Day was a week after my lung surgery. Father Joe Tetlow came over to say a Mass for us. That touched my heart deeply. Then I sat on the couch and supervised the cooking in the kitchen. I was not allowed to go into the kitchen at all.

My children did all of the cooking and my grandchildren did all of the cleaning up after our delicious Thanksgiving meal. We had a repeat for Christmas dinner. I was so filled with love and gratitude. God once again provided the graces for me and my family to get through a very difficult few months. One of the gifts to me was learning to receive!

As 2009 rolled around I slowly began to get back into the swing of life, though at a limited pace. I returned to art class and to seeing my Directees and Clients. The fatigue kept me from doing little else. I had to go at a much slower pace than before. I was so grateful to be working again. Then on Mothers' Day the in-town kids and Bob took me out for lunch. Greg was working at the time and could not join us. After lunch Bob, D and I drove out to the Airport to see Greg at the Fire Station. I had made a batch of brownies for the Firemen and Paramedics and was carrying them as we walked up to meet Greg's co-workers. I extended my hand to one of them and stepped to the left to meet the next guy when all of a sudden I found myself dancing across the driveway in front of the ambulance. I thought I was on flat ground but had stepped off where the curb was narrowing. The brownies went flying one way and I ended up falling on my left side as five Paramedics stood there watching along with Bob and D. The brownies landed intact but I did not. I can testify that Press N' Seal really does work. Too bad I was not wrapped in it! I instinctively knew that I had broken my hip. Of course, I got immediate attention. I was given "happy juice" and placed in the ambulance. My very own Paramedic son Greg rode in the back with me. He said, "Gee, Mom, this is a first!" I replied, "It had better be the last, too!" I really gifted the Paramedics in that they always get to an accident after it happens. This time they got to see the accident happen. Besides, I did not have to wait for an ambulance and help!!!!!!! You see, there is a gift in everything!!!!!!!

I don't remember much about the ER except I heard them say that they were going to have to cut my slacks off. I heard D tell then that I would be upset because my slacks were brand new. I managed to tell them not to cut them off. The nurse said it would hurt me when they removed them. I told her I was already in pain and I could take it. The x-rays showed I had crushed the top of the femur into the hip and would have to have surgery. There were five pieces of shattered bone where the femur goes into the hip socket. Blood tests revealed that I was too anemic for immediate surgery and would have to have a transfusion first.

I really don't remember much that first night. I know that Greg spent the night in my room. The next day I was given two transfusions to prepare for surgery the following day. I was not taken into surgery until 5 p.m. on Tuesday. I don't remember spending the next two days in ICU. Even though Bob was not a Chaplain at Baylor Grapevine he wore his Chaplain's badge so that he could just walk into ICU any time. He sneaked into ICU to see me with the nurse's approval.

I had hallucinations when I went to my room. I told Bob that I needed to go to Chick Fil A but I could not get out of bed. Then I told him that he did not live in Oak Cliff. I was aware of saying these things but I did not make sense. It had to be the strong pain medication I was on at the time. Two physical therapists came in the fourth day to get me up. The pain brought tears to my eyes. I had a rod from my hip down the femur to right before my knee. Then I had a large screw holding my crushed femur and hip bone together along with two smaller screws. I thought I would never be able to walk again. The following Monday I was transferred by ambulance to Dallas Medical Center where I would undergo physical therapy for the next 10 days. The saying, "No pain, no gain!" is really true. I had physical therapy three times each day. It was painful but it worked. Walking finally became less painful.

I got a copy of the x-ray when I returned to the orthopedic surgeon and learned that the large screw holding my femur and hip together was sticking out from the bone. The surgeon said that he could not fix it without having to redo the entire leg and he did not want to do that. I could not bear another major surgery so I have lived with the pain for almost six years now. A second opinion confirmed the original surgeon's opinion. I recently had terrible pain in the hip and had difficulty walking. X-rays showed bursitis. The bursa was drained and I was given a cortisone shot. It helped for about two weeks and the pain returned. I get very discouraged at times when I cannot walk too far. Walking a mall on a shopping trip with the girls is out. I have had to make many adjustments to my life. I don't always want to drink of the cup I have been handed but God gives me the grace to accept what is.

Within a few months after the hip surgery I had a bout with pneumonia and was hospitalized again for 8 days of antibiotic IV's. The next two years I was hospitalized three more times with pneumonia. I spent 8 days each time. Sometime in between those hospital stays I had a stomach virus, which dehydrated me so I ended up in the hospital again for three days. I developed Premature Ventricular Contractions (PVC's) and thought my heart would jump right out of my chest. I was exhausted again and getting discouraged as I wondered if this was how I would spend the rest of my life. I pleaded with God to heal me! I was so weary of dealing with health issues. I was back in the hospital with pneumonia again just a few months later. I was diagnosed with two lung infections that are difficult to eradicate. I was told that I would have to take three very powerful antibiotics for 12 to 18 months. Fortunately, I am not contagious. The infections are in the scarred part of my right lung, which was damaged by radiation therapy 34 years ago. Radiation also damaged my shoulder blade, part of my heart and part of my liver. So here I am – a physical mess!!!!!!!! I have just been taken off of the three antibiotics I had been on for the past 13 months. My concern is that I might have to take antibiotics indefinitely since the infections cannot be completely eradicated. I certainly do not want to be hospitalized every few months with pneumonia. The side effects from the medications are tolerable. I am also a diabetic; have neuropathy that has moved up from my feet to my hips; loss of balance as a result; bronchiectasis; and lymphedema in my right arm. "You just can't keep a good woman down," as someone said to me! I am a good woman who is also stubborn and has the gift of perseverance. I am grateful to the Lord for this!

Somewhere in the midst of my frequent hospital stays I had a partially torn rotator cuff in my right arm. A can of condensed milk had exploded in my kitchen as it was being boiled to make caramel. The entire ceiling, floor, cabinets and appliances were covered with tiny pieces of caramel. We enlisted the help of our kids. I was right there with Bob and the kids scrapping and cleaning the awful mess. I overdid it and tore the rotator cuff. When I finally went to the doctor a few days later, I was relieved to know that I did not need surgery, only physical therapy. I was becoming a pro at physical therapy.

Then a few months later I was eating dinner when I choked on peas. I have trouble swallowing at times since the stroke. Bob was at the hospital at a dinner meeting so I was alone. I could not breathe and became terrified so I rammed my stomach on the corner of the table. It did not work, so I rammed it again harder, ended up throwing up and could now breathe. I told Bob what had happened when he came home later. While I was getting ready for bed, I became lightheaded and very weak. I called to Bob to help me. He got me to bed and took my blood pressure. It was 88/40. I decided that I was just in shock from the choking episode and would see how I felt in the morning. It was my week-end to teach at Perkins so I pulled myself up by the bootstraps and taught Friday, Saturday and Sunday. I did not feel well but I have the ability to block out what I am feeling and function. My mother trained me that way! The dizziness had gone away so I thought I would be OK. The BP had come up, too! However, the pain and tenderness in my left side were not going away. So I called the Gastroenterologist on Tuesday. I went in a couple of days later when he could see me. He said it was probably Irritable Bowel Syndrome and all I had to do was follow his regimen for it. I somehow knew that something was wrong and insisted on a CAT Scan. The doctor had egg on his face when the Scan showed that I had had internal bleeding in my abdomen as a result of a lacerated spleen. There were several dried blood pockets in my abdomen. The gift in it was if I had gone to the ER the night it happened, I would have ended up in surgery. Now a week later the laceration was healing. The danger in it was that I could have bled to death. God was once again taking care of me. Discerning the right call is not always easy! I am grateful to God for the outcome of this episode! I constantly pray for the grace and wisdom to pay attention to my body and to make the right call.

In spite of all of this, I am still working. I see my Directees, have about three clients since I gave up doing therapy two years ago; am a Court-Appointed Expert for the Dallas Diocesan Marriage Tribunal, where I do annulment work and marriage-readiness work – about three or four cases per year. I have trained Spiritual Directors at Perkins School of Theology at SMU three week-ends per year for the past five plus years and grade homework and verbatims in between the week-end classes; and I teach classes at Montserrat Retreat House for the Ignatian Spirituality Institute. Every two years I also help train Jesuits, Ministers and Lay People in how to give Preached Retreats. I recently gave up doing week-end retreats at Montserrat and now will do just an occasional Saturday there. I have cut back, though it may not seem that way! God gives me the strength and grace to keep doing His work. He will let me know when it is time to fold up my tent. In the meantime I will keep on keepin' on! I have been so blessed to have been called to these ministries!

The health issues continue to plague me. I long for the days when I felt great and had lots of energy to accomplish things. The two graces I ask for daily are the grace to accept what is and the grace to surrender my life and my all to God. I am grateful for the 81 years God has given me. All the trials and tribulations I have experienced since I was born have brought me to the place I am today. My Ignatian training has allowed me to find God in all things. I pray that my story will give you hope and the courage to keep going when life gives you challenges.

I know that God wanted me to be born and that He loves me as I am and constantly invites me into a deeper relationship with Him. I don't always understand His ways, but I have lived long enough to know that "All things work together for good to those who love the Lord and are called according to His purpose." (Romans 8:28) I can testify to that Scripture. My daily prayer is, "Lord, please give me a loving, willing, grateful, forgiving, and listening heart today and help me to be a blessing to the people in my life." I pray that my story blesses you in some way.

As I look back on my 81 years of life I certainly can see God at work. There have been many joys, many mountain tops as well as many sorrows and deep valleys. I know that I know that I know that He has always been with me, carrying me when I could not walk; encouraging me through the people He put in my life; giving me courage when I did not think I could keep going; blessing me at every turn; recycling my garbage into grace; and showing me His love in so many ways, and through so many people in my life. I don't know what the future holds and would not want to know if I could. But what I do know is that I will keep "Stepping Out in Faith One Slat at a Time" until it is my time to paint rainbows with God in Heaven!

About the Author

§

ELIZABETH (LIZ) TAYLOR MOULIN HOLDS a B.A. Degree in Education with Endorsements in Language/Learning Disabilities, Early Childhood Education, Kindergarten and a Minor in Sociology. She has a Master of Education Degree in Special Education and Certification as an Educational Diagnostician and Supervisor. Her Master of Arts Degree is in Counseling and Guidance. She received her degrees from Texas Women's University. She is a Licensed Professional Counselor; a Licensed Marriage and Family Therapist; a Spiritual Director; a Retreat Director at Montserrat Jesuit Retreat House in Lake Dallas; a Court Appointed Expert for the Diocese of Dallas Marriage Tribunal. Liz also gives talks, workshops, missions, trains Spiritual Directors at Perkins School of Theology at SMU and also trains Retreat Directors and teaches classes for the Ignatian Spirituality Institute at Montserrat.

On a personal note, Liz has been married to the love of her life, Bob, for 60 years. They have been blessed with four wonderful children and their spouses: Tara (Moulin) and Joe Arciniega; Chris and Danene (Hasz) Moulin; Lisa (Moulin) Kupersmith; and Greg and Danita(D)

(Littlefield) Moulin. They are blessed with seven grandchildren: Emily (Arciniega) and Jesse Lashbrook, Adam & Melissa (Richel) Arciniega, Alex Arciniega, Michael and Becca (McGonagill) Moulin, Matt and Rebecca (Stewart) Moulin, Kelsey (Moulin) and Blake Martin, Forrest and Leticia (Moura) Moulin. Great-Grandchildren Jessica and

Faith Elizabeth Moulin, Landry Grace and Levi Joseph Lashbrook and Anna Gabriela Moulin. Berkleigh Elizabeth Martin will complete the picture in April, 2016.

Liz is the author of three books:

A Handbook for Parents of Early Childhood Handicapped Children – 1980
On Becoming a Butterfly, 2012 – An allegory about her life.
The Psychotherapy of Wholeness: A Comparison of Redecision Therapy and Ignatian Spiritual Exercises, 2014 - Co-Authored with Dr. Linda Carmicle.

Reviews of the Book

§

Though I have known Liz Moulin for five years and spoken with her many times about her life and experiences, I was still surprised by what I read in her memoirs. They are literally a page-turner, something I found difficult to put down. Liz has had an amazing life, with many sorrows and many joys, always supported by her strong faith in God's care for her. This is an inspiring book.

Fr. Billy Huete, S.J.
Rector of Jesuit Community –
Loyola University
New Orleans, Louisiana

In *Stepping Out in Faith One Slat at a Time* Elizabeth (Liz) Moulin offers her readers a window into the journey of faith, the wisdom of an accomplished director and therapist, and a witness to the grace of God. Read it to be encouraged, read it for companionship, read it for healing, and find in its pages an image for the spiritual life that will sustain you on your journey.

Frederick W. Schmidt
Rueben P. Job Chair in Spiritual Formation
Garrett-Evangelical Theological Seminary
And author of *The Dave Test*

Elizabeth Taylor Moulin is the modern version of the wise and virtuous woman described in Proverbs 31. She gives vivid descriptions of a young wife whose resilience and determination enable her to find a medical solution for her seriously ill daughter. Liz developed a strong character as a child with an alcoholic father. She sought strength through the nuns who taught her about faith and the love of God. Her faith in God, her intelligence and her tenacity enabled her to finish graduate school while juggling the demands of home, four young children and her husband's job loss. Even breast cancer could not defeat Liz, who is a 34-year cancer survivor. Her graphic descriptions of a graduate student mom drew me back to my own early experiences. This is a good read for any woman searching for answers in a busy world.

Linda Harper Carmicle, Ph.D.

This is a story – a true story – that harmonizes the major chords of a life: Faith, family, calling, and health. Liz Moulin shares her life in what I would call the "naïve style": Fully transparent and free of guile. The essence of her story is a ceaseless faith in Christ as Lord and Savior. Her early childhood captures Jesus' message: "I tell you the truth, anyone who will not receive the Kingdom of God like a little child will never enter it." (Mark 10:15) Liz was born into a stressed, struggling family that endowed her with enough adverse childhood experiences to crush spirit and soul. Not so with Liz. Her temperament was "gifted" by God (that is the way she would put it and I agree) with traits of persistence, conscientiousness, and intelligence. Better yet, she found her way to Our Lady of Prompt Succor Catholic School (what an appropriate name!) and the Sisters of Mt. Carmel. Organized religion is often disparaged in the popular culture of today and the Roman Catholic Church has had to deal with its share of the same. Read this story! People of faith rise to the occasion! Sisters and priests do what they are called to do and what Christians are supposed to do – strive to live a Christ-like life.

Elizabeth Moulin took the succor provided by her church and its sisters and infused it into her family life as a wife, mother, and grandmother. The same with her professional life through her work as a teacher, therapist, and spiritual director. From the story of her life we see that trust and faith in our Trinitarian God can arc across a lifetime and not be corroded by adversity, stress or loss. I found it moving and ironic that the faith that sustained her when she was traumatized by parental dysfunction would find its way back, through the grace God had given her, to those very same parents. Here is a story where victimization does not produce a victim; where God-loving people make all the difference in the world; and where the recipient of both responds with gratitude and grace.

Edgar Nace, M.D.
Clinical Professor of Psychiatry
University of Texas Southwestern Medical School

The power of the Holy Spirit to change lives is so evident in this wonderful story of redemption. Through struggles and joys, the indomitable human spirit comes alive. We are saddened, enlightened, and brought to eventual peace through Liz's wonderful telling of her story.

Ron Boudreaux, S.J.
Director – Montserrat Jesuit Retreat House
Lake Dallas, Texas 75065

Made in the USA
Coppell, TX
16 January 2022